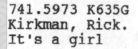

IT'S A
GIRL

To: _____

From: _____

IT'S A GIRL

A BABY BLUES® BOOK

by Rick Kirkman and Jerry Scott

**Andrews McMeel
Publishing, LLC**

Kansas City • Sydney • London

Baby Blues® is syndicated internation
information, write King Features Syndic
New York, New York 10019.

 For information, write Andrews McMeel Publishing, LLC, an Andrews McMeel Universal company, 1130 Walnut Street, Kansas City, Missouri 64106.

10 11 12 13 14 WKT 10 9 8 7 6 5 4 3 2 1

ISBN-13: 978-0-7407-9167-3
ISBN-10: 0-7407-9167-2

Library of Congress Control Number: 2009936123

www.andrewsmcmeel.com

Find *Baby Blues*® on the Web at
www.babyblues.com.

ATTENTION: SCHOOLS AND BUSINESSES
Andrews McMeel books are available at quantity discounts with bulk purchase for educational, business, or sales promotional use. For information, please write to: Special Sales Department, Andrews McMeel Publishing, LLC, 1130 Walnut Street, Kansas City, Missouri 64106.

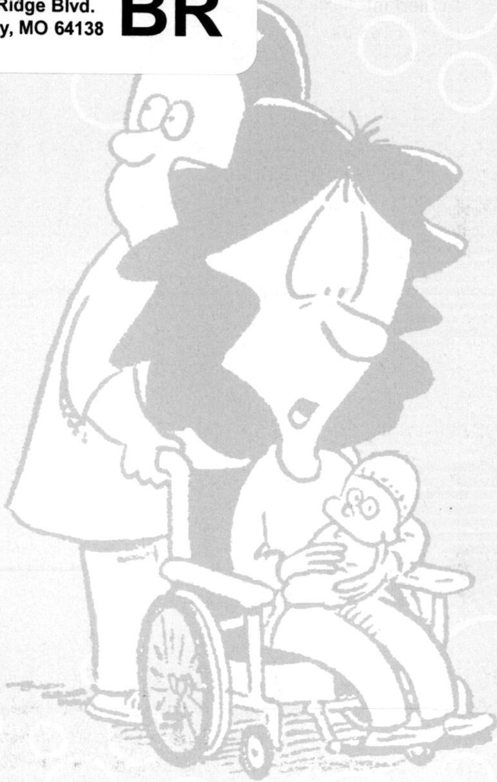

CHAPTER 1

PREGNANCY

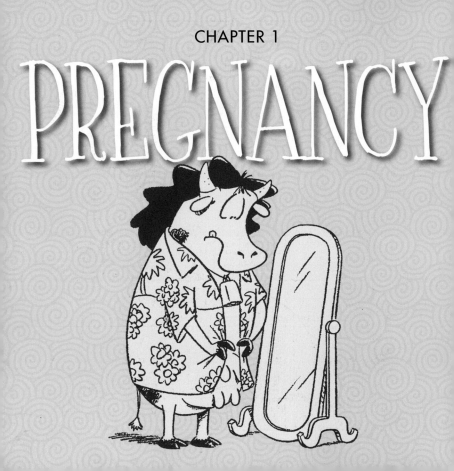

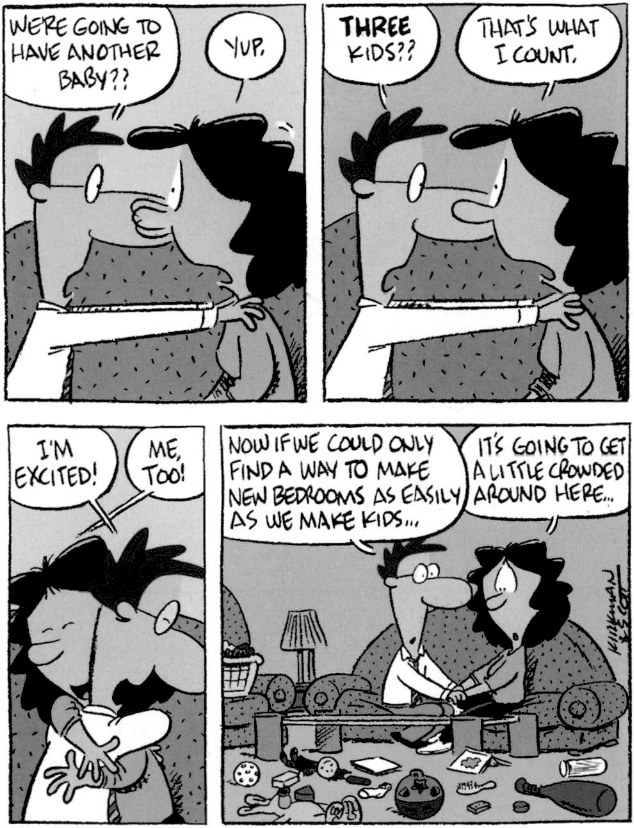
WE'RE GOING TO HAVE ANOTHER BABY??
YUP.
THREE KIDS??
THAT'S WHAT I COUNT.
I'M EXCITED!
ME, TOO!
NOW IF WE COULD ONLY FIND A WAY TO MAKE NEW BEDROOMS AS EASILY AS WE MAKE KIDS...
IT'S GOING TO GET A LITTLE CROWDED AROUND HERE...

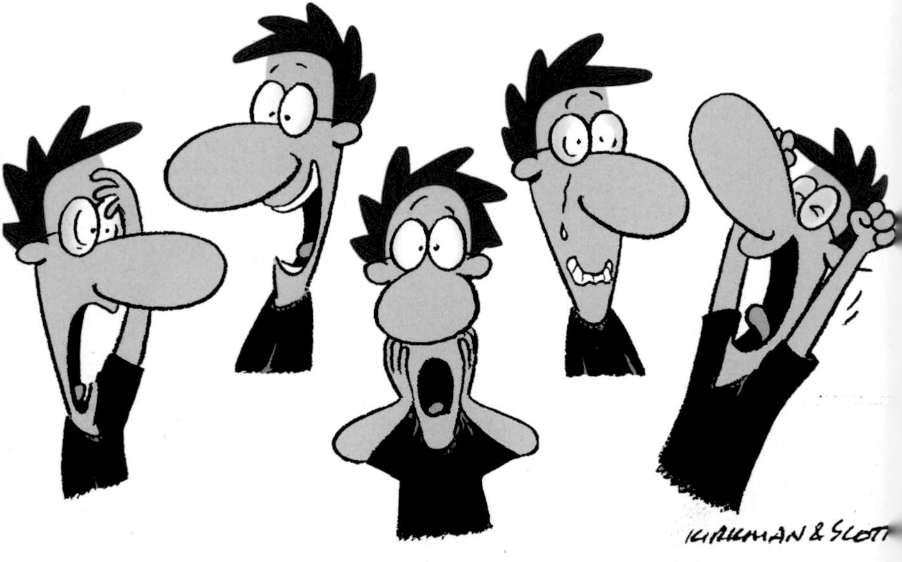
KIRKMAN & SCOTT

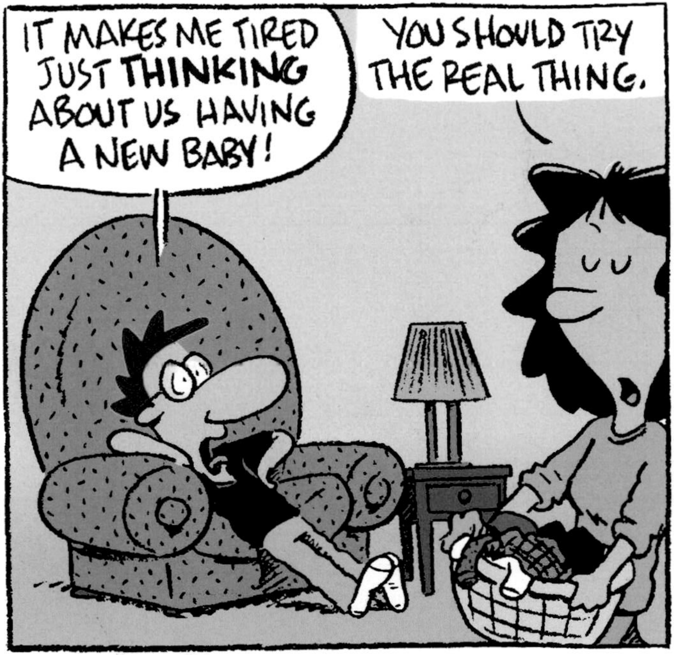
IT MAKES ME TIRED JUST **THINKING** ABOUT US HAVING A NEW BABY!
YOU SHOULD TRY THE REAL THING.

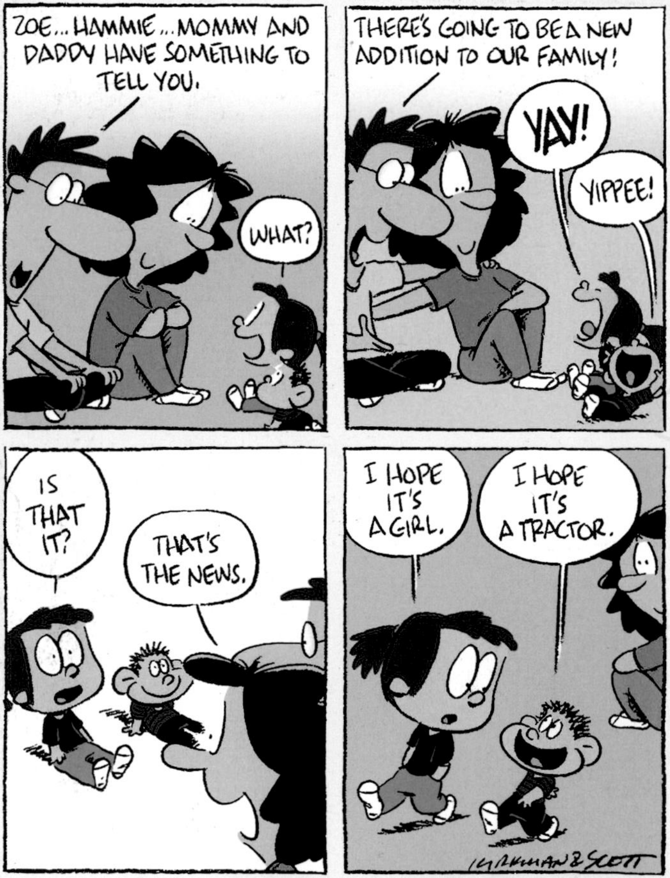
ZOE... HAMMIE... MOMMY AND DADDY HAVE SOMETHING TO TELL YOU.
WHAT?
THERE'S GOING TO BE A NEW ADDITION TO OUR FAMILY!
YAY!
YIPPEE!
IS THAT IT?
THAT'S THE NEWS.
I HOPE IT'S A GIRL.
I HOPE IT'S A TRACTOR.
KIRKMAN & SCOTT

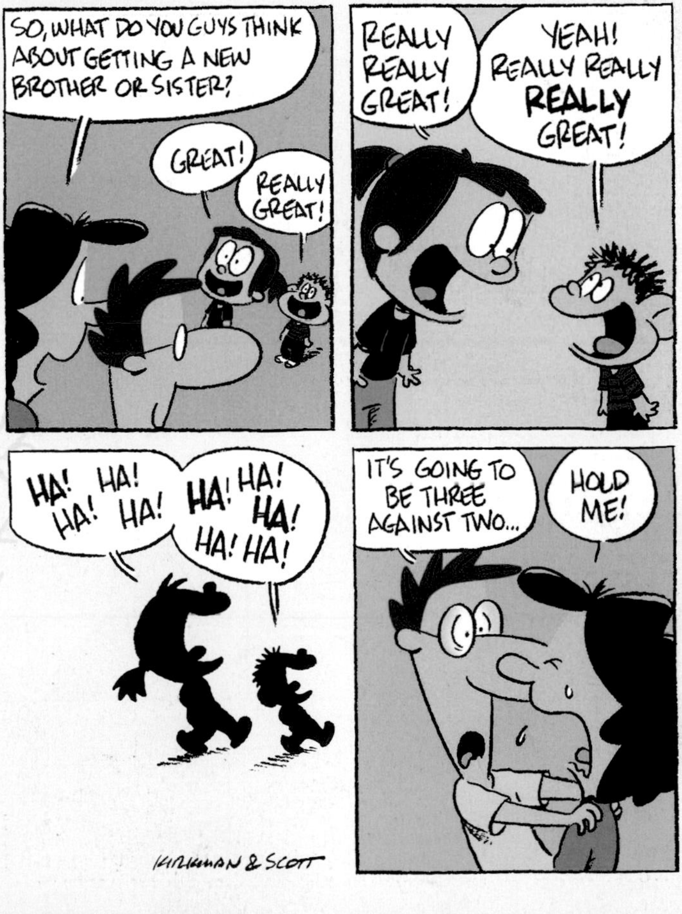
SO, WHAT DO YOU GUYS THINK ABOUT GETTING A NEW BROTHER OR SISTER?
GREAT!
REALLY GREAT!
REALLY REALLY GREAT!
YEAH! REALLY REALLY REALLY GREAT!
HA! HA! HA! HA!
HA! HA! HA! HA! HA!
IT'S GOING TO BE THREE AGAINST TWO...
HOLD ME!
KIRKMAN & SCOTT

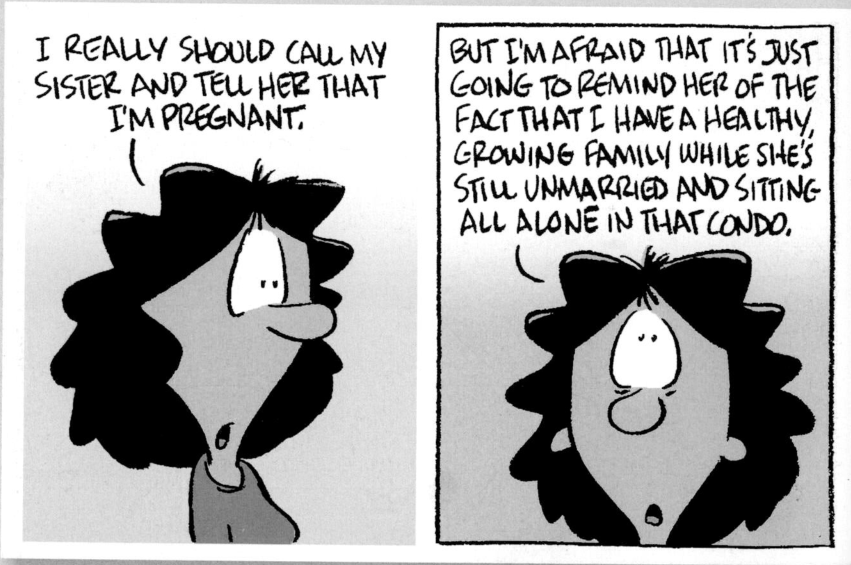
I REALLY SHOULD CALL MY SISTER AND TELL HER THAT I'M PREGNANT.
BUT I'M AFRAID THAT IT'S JUST GOING TO REMIND HER OF THE FACT THAT I HAVE A HEALTHY, GROWING FAMILY WHILE SHE'S STILL UNMARRIED AND SITTING ALL ALONE IN THAT CONDO.

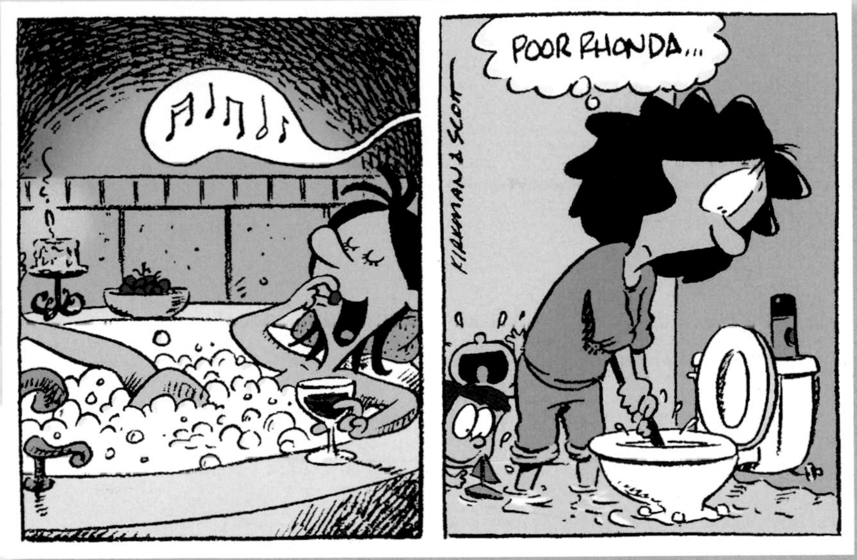
POOR RHONDA...
KIRKMAN & SCOTT

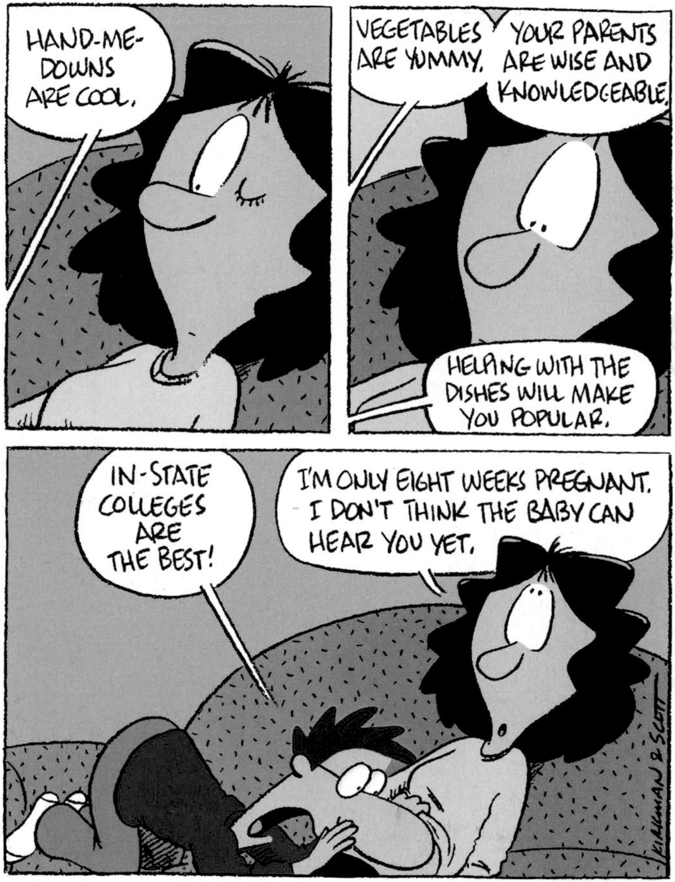
HAND-ME-DOWNS ARE COOL.
VEGETABLES ARE YUMMY.
YOUR PARENTS ARE WISE AND KNOWLEDGEABLE.
HELPING WITH THE DISHES WILL MAKE YOU POPULAR.
IN-STATE COLLEGES ARE THE BEST!
I'M ONLY EIGHT WEEKS PREGNANT. I DON'T THINK THE BABY CAN HEAR YOU YET.
KIRKMAN & SCOTT

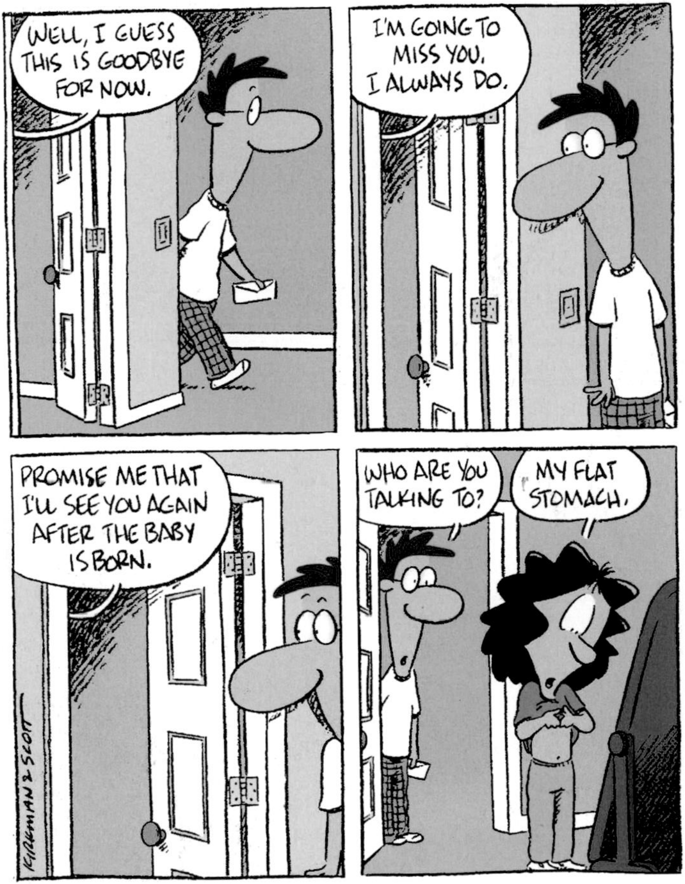
WELL, I GUESS THIS IS GOODBYE FOR NOW.
I'M GOING TO MISS YOU. I ALWAYS DO.
PROMISE ME THAT I'LL SEE YOU AGAIN AFTER THE BABY IS BORN.
KIRKMAN & SCOTT
WHO ARE YOU TALKING TO?
MY FLAT STOMACH.

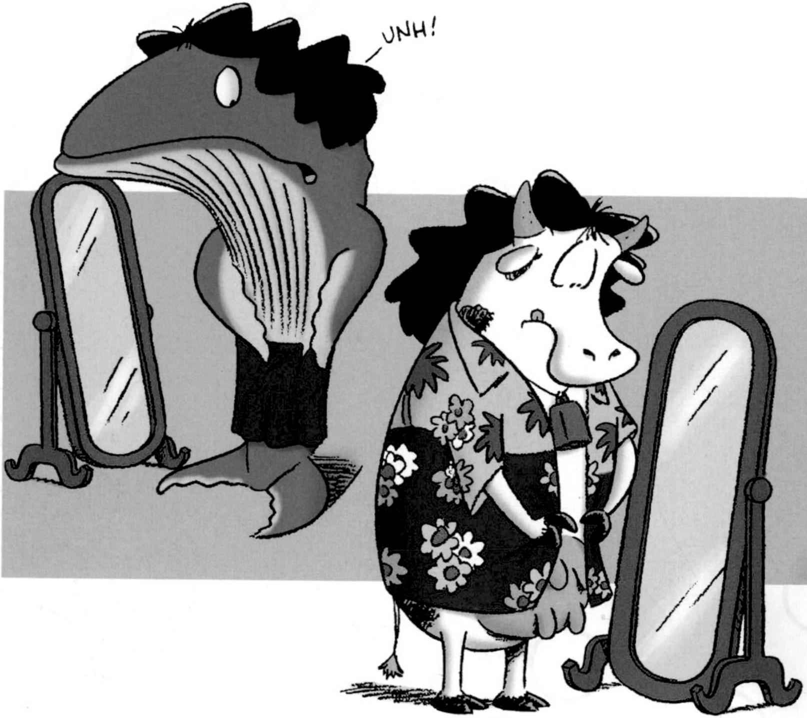
UNH!

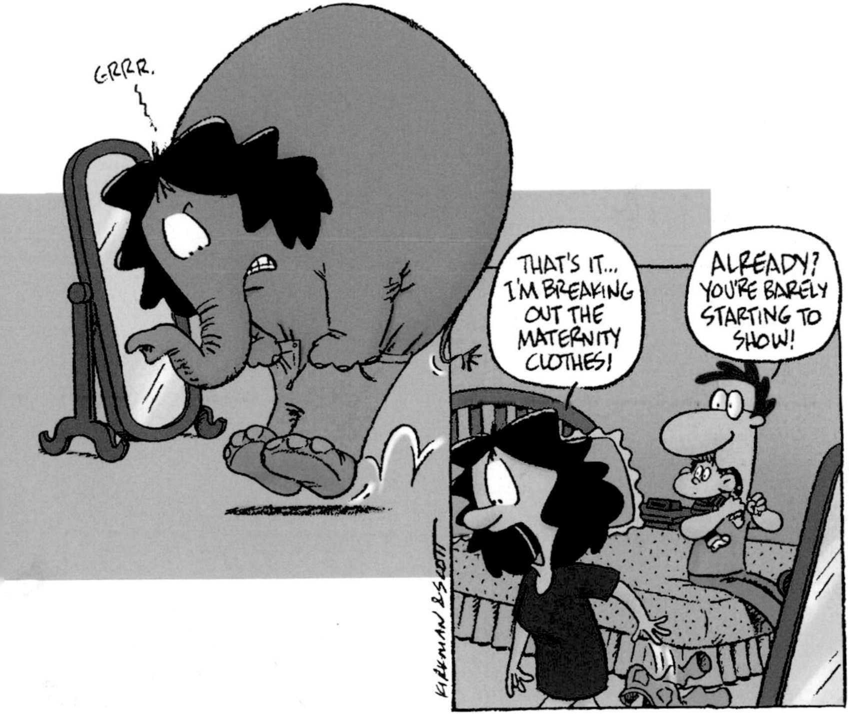
GRRR.
THAT'S IT... I'M BREAKING OUT THE MATERNITY CLOTHES!
ALREADY? YOU'RE BARELY STARTING TO SHOW!
KIRKMAN & SCOTT

The Third Month
Your body is working overtime building a baby, so it's important to treat it right.

Eat well, exercise moderately...

YAWN!

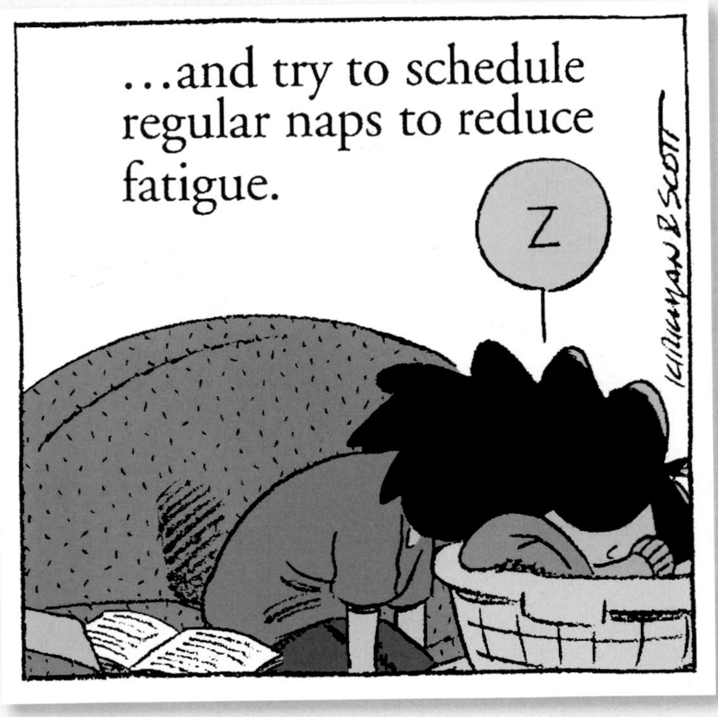
...and try to schedule regular naps to reduce fatigue.
Z
KIRKMAN & SCOTT

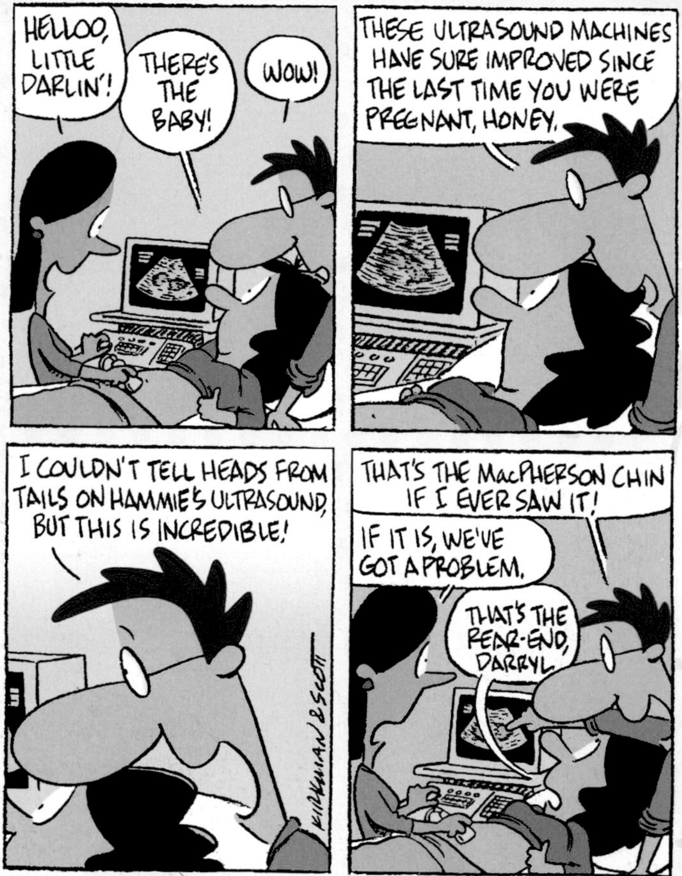
HELLOO, LITTLE DARLIN'!
THERE'S THE BABY!
WOW!
THESE ULTRASOUND MACHINES HAVE SURE IMPROVED SINCE THE LAST TIME YOU WERE PREGNANT, HONEY.
I COULDN'T TELL HEADS FROM TAILS ON HAMMIE'S ULTRASOUND, BUT THIS IS INCREDIBLE!
KIRKMAN & SCOTT
THAT'S THE MacPHERSON CHIN IF I EVER SAW IT!
IF IT IS, WE'VE GOT A PROBLEM.
THAT'S THE REAR-END, DARRYL.

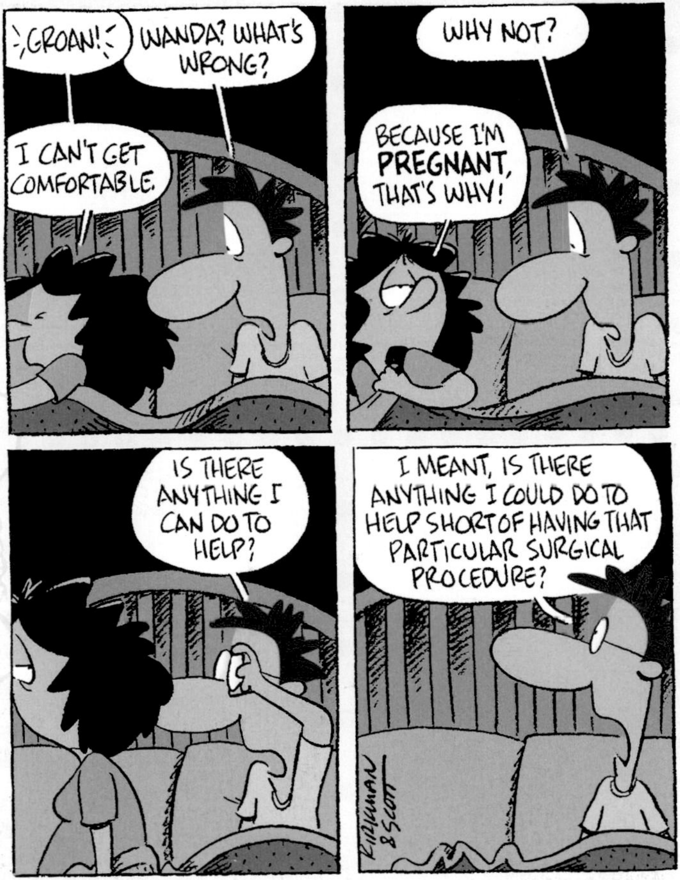
GROAN!
WANDA? WHAT'S WRONG?
I CAN'T GET COMFORTABLE.
WHY NOT?
BECAUSE I'M **PREGNANT**, THAT'S WHY!
IS THERE ANYTHING I CAN DO TO HELP?
I MEANT, IS THERE ANYTHING I COULD DO TO HELP SHORT OF HAVING THAT PARTICULAR SURGICAL PROCEDURE?
KIRKMAN & SCOTT

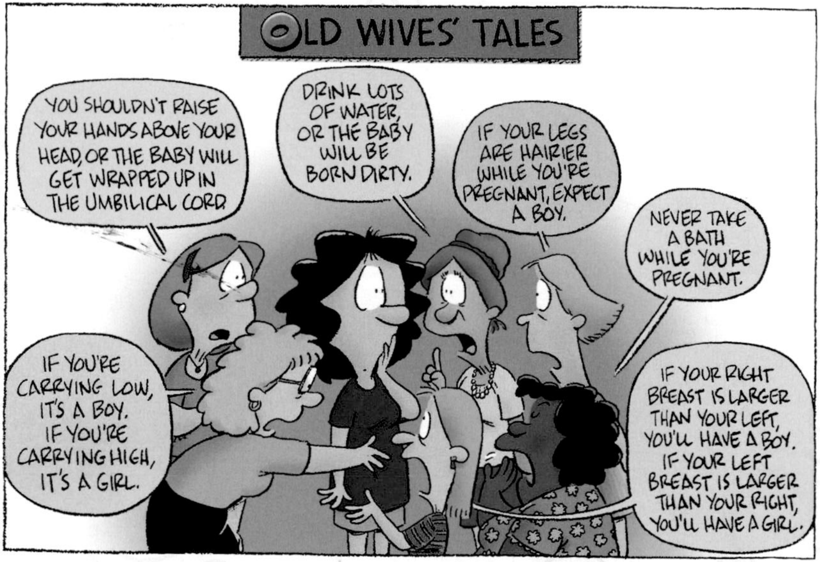
OLD WIVES' TALES
YOU SHOULDN'T RAISE YOUR HANDS ABOVE YOUR HEAD, OR THE BABY WILL GET WRAPPED UP IN THE UMBILICAL CORD.
DRINK LOTS OF WATER, OR THE BABY WILL BE BORN DIRTY.
IF YOUR LEGS ARE HAIRIER WHILE YOU'RE PREGNANT, EXPECT A BOY.
NEVER TAKE A BATH WHILE YOU'RE PREGNANT.
IF YOU'RE CARRYING LOW, IT'S A BOY. IF YOU'RE CARRYING HIGH, IT'S A GIRL.
IF YOUR RIGHT BREAST IS LARGER THAN YOUR LEFT, YOU'LL HAVE A BOY. IF YOUR LEFT BREAST IS LARGER THAN YOUR RIGHT, YOU'LL HAVE A GIRL.

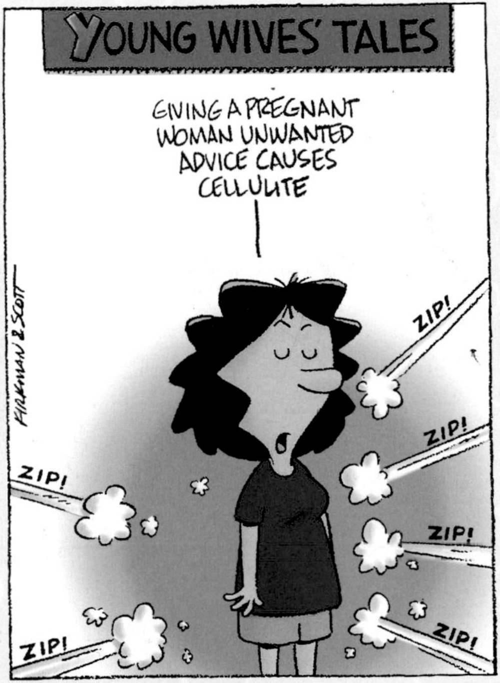
YOUNG WIVES' TALES
GIVING A PREGNANT WOMAN UNWANTED ADVICE CAUSES CELLULITE
KIRKMAN & SCOTT
ZIP!
ZIP!
ZIP!
ZIP!
ZIP!
ZIP!

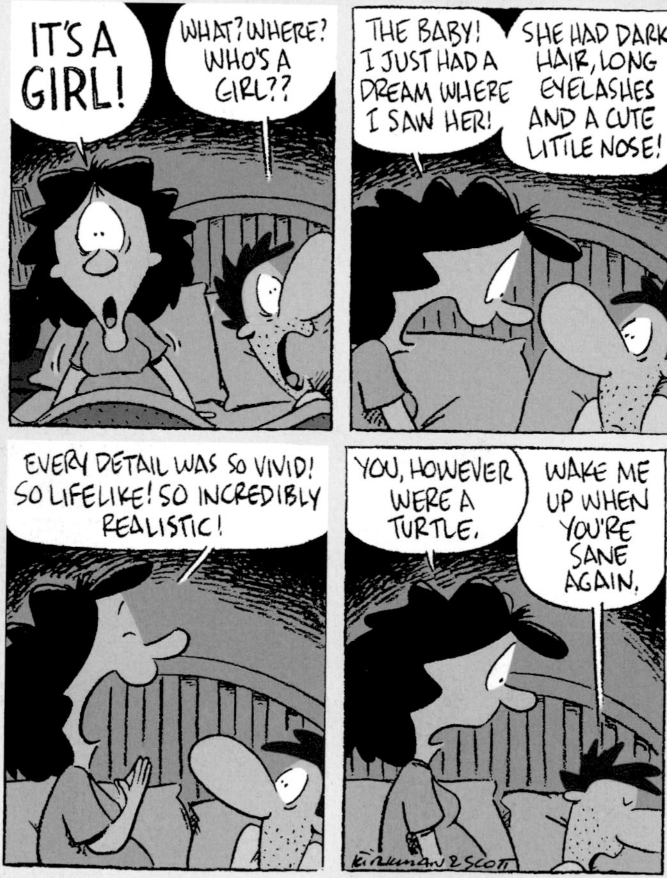
IT'S A GIRL!
WHAT? WHERE? WHO'S A GIRL??
THE BABY! I JUST HAD A DREAM WHERE I SAW HER!
SHE HAD DARK HAIR, LONG EYELASHES AND A CUTE LITTLE NOSE!
EVERY DETAIL WAS SO VIVID! SO LIFELIKE! SO INCREDIBLY REALISTIC!
YOU, HOWEVER WERE A TURTLE.
WAKE ME UP WHEN YOU'RE SANE AGAIN.
KIRKMAN & SCOTT

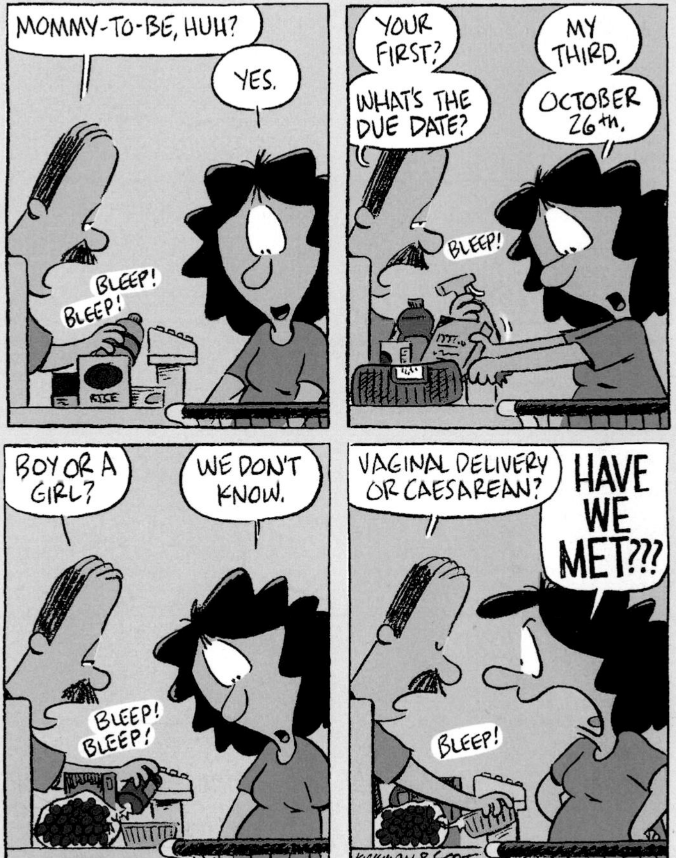
MOMMY-TO-BE, HUH?
YES.
BLEEP!
BLEEP!
YOUR FIRST?
MY THIRD.
WHAT'S THE DUE DATE?
OCTOBER 26th.
BLEEP!
BOY OR A GIRL?
WE DON'T KNOW.
BLEEP!
BLEEP!
VAGINAL DELIVERY OR CAESAREAN?
HAVE WE MET???
BLEEP!
KIRKMAN & SCOTT

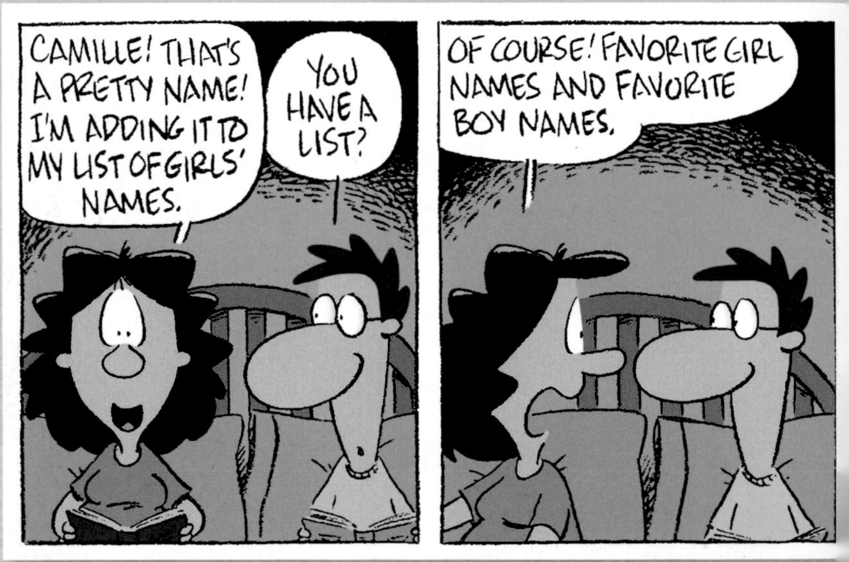
CAMILLE! THAT'S A PRETTY NAME! I'M ADDING IT TO MY LIST OF GIRLS' NAMES.
YOU HAVE A LIST?
OF COURSE! FAVORITE GIRL NAMES AND FAVORITE BOY NAMES.

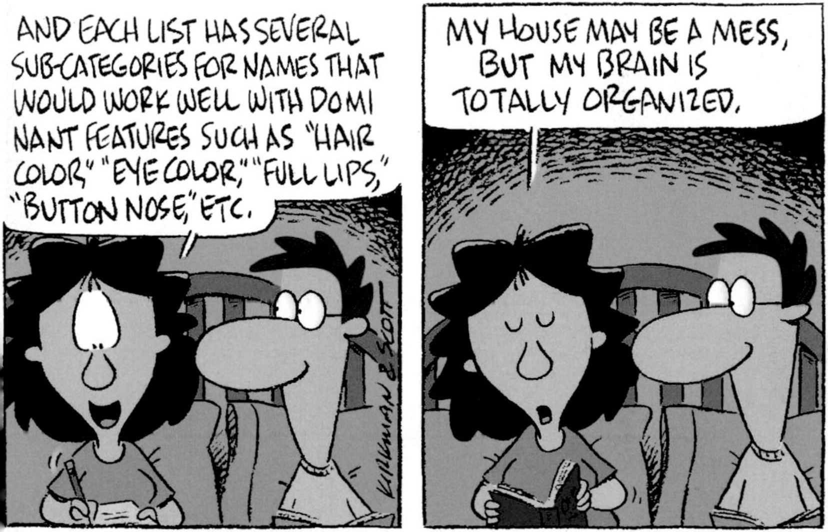
AND EACH LIST HAS SEVERAL SUB-CATEGORIES FOR NAMES THAT WOULD WORK WELL WITH DOMI NANT FEATURES SUCH AS "HAIR COLOR" "EYE COLOR," "FULL LIPS," "BUTTON NOSE," ETC.
KIRKMAN & SCOTT
MY HOUSE MAY BE A MESS, BUT MY BRAIN IS TOTALLY ORGANIZED.

CHAPTER 2

BIRTH

EXTRA INSURANCE
COLLEGE FUND
WIPES
PAMPIES
PAMPIES DIAPERS

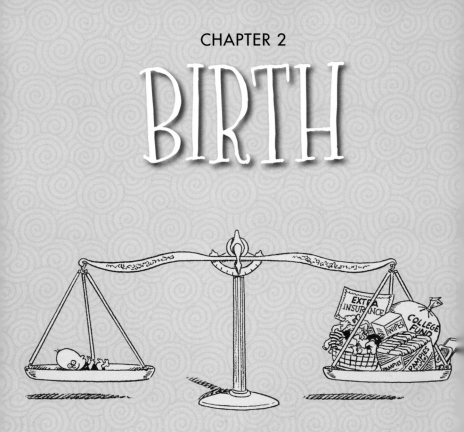

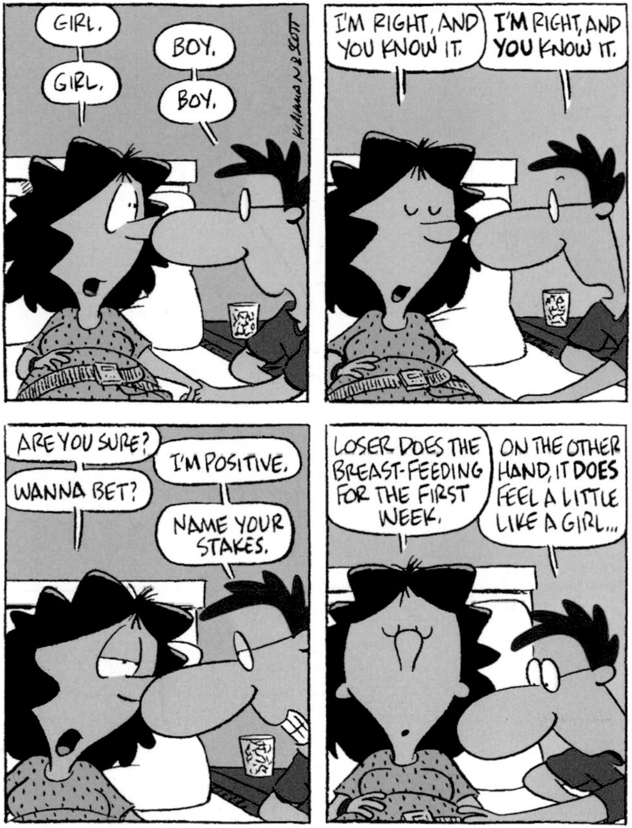
GIRL.
BOY.
GIRL.
BOY.
KIRKMAN & SCOTT
I'M RIGHT, AND YOU KNOW IT.
I'M RIGHT, AND YOU KNOW IT.
ARE YOU SURE?
I'M POSITIVE.
WANNA BET?
NAME YOUR STAKES.
LOSER DOES THE BREAST-FEEDING FOR THE FIRST WEEK.
ON THE OTHER HAND, IT **DOES** FEEL A LITTLE LIKE A GIRL...

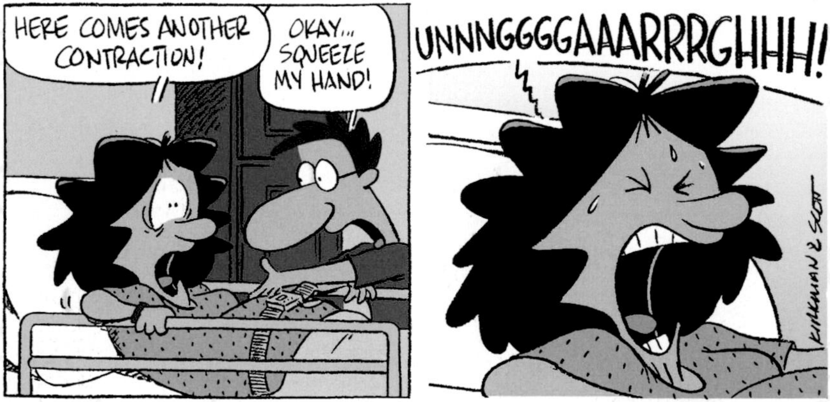
HERE COMES ANOTHER CONTRACTION!
OKAY... SQUEEZE MY HAND!
UNNNGGGGAAARRRRGHHH!
KIRKMAN & SCOTT

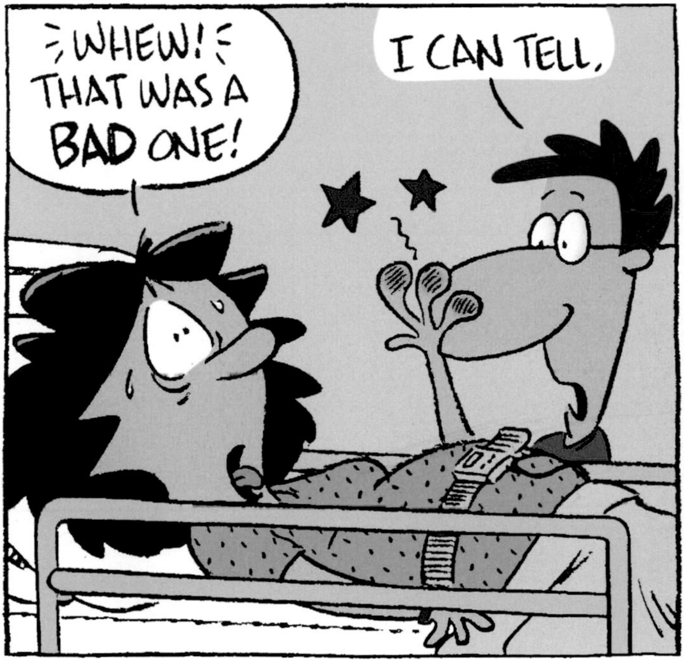
WHEW! THAT WAS A BAD ONE!
I CAN TELL.

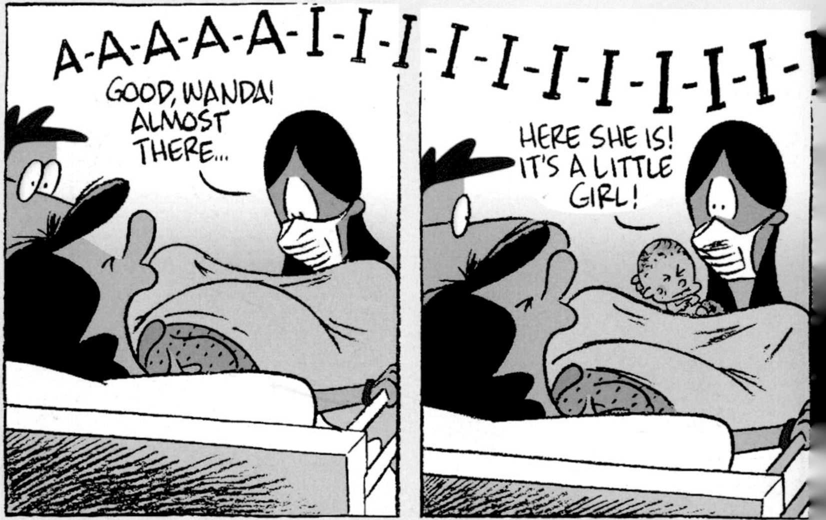
A-A-A-A-A-I-I-I-I-I-I-I-I-I-I-
GOOD, WANDA! ALMOST THERE...
HERE SHE IS! IT'S A LITTLE GIRL!

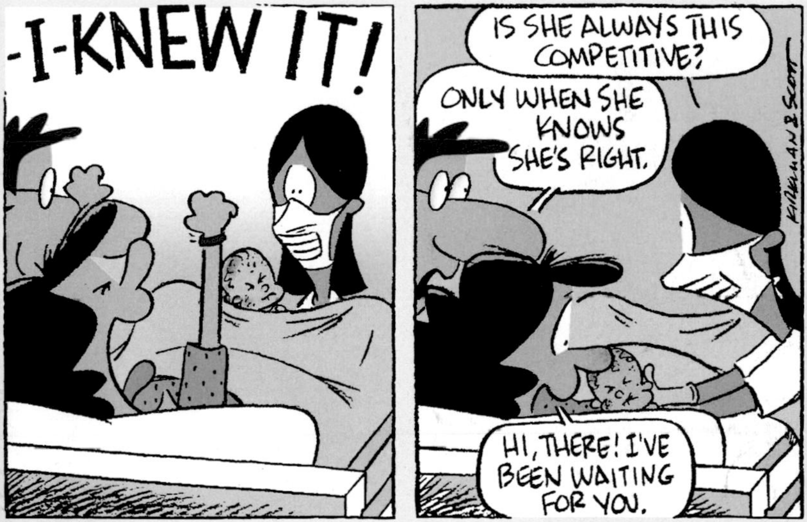
-I-KNEW IT!
IS SHE ALWAYS THIS COMPETITIVE?
ONLY WHEN SHE KNOWS SHE'S RIGHT.
HI, THERE! I'VE BEEN WAITING FOR YOU.

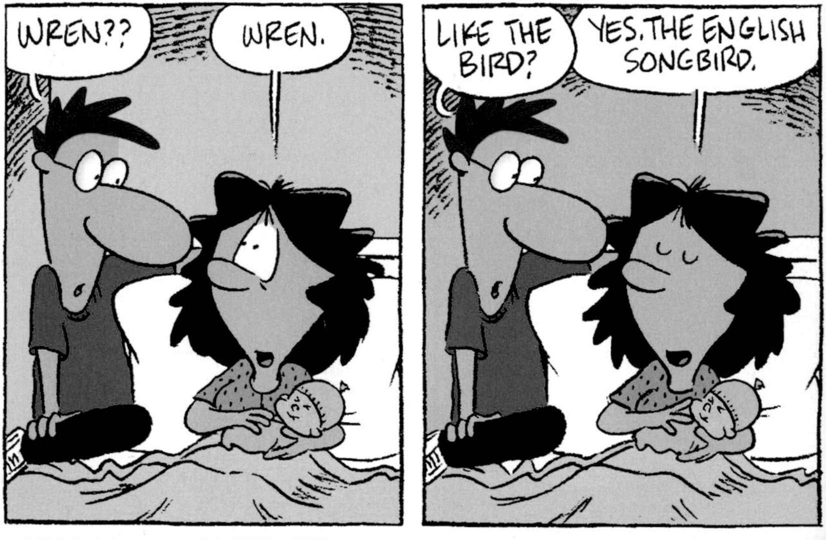
WREN??
WREN.
LIKE THE BIRD?
YES. THE ENGLISH SONGBIRD.

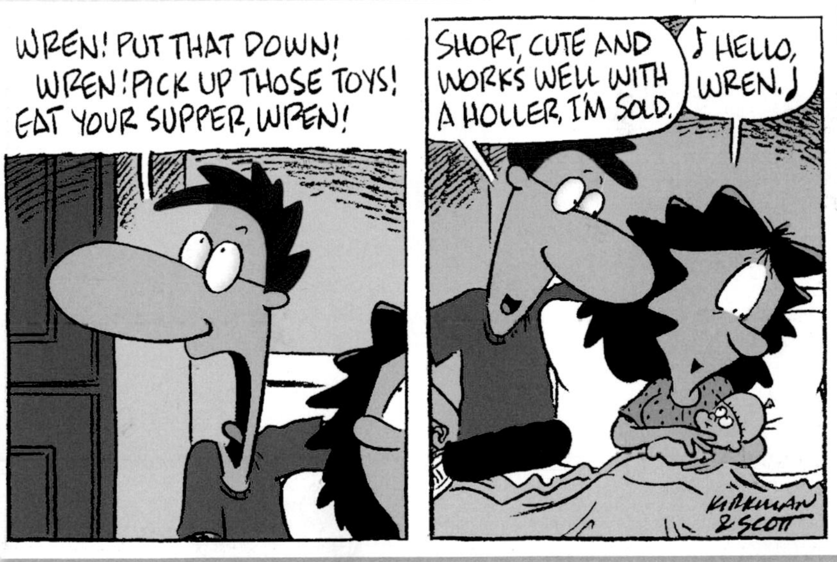
WREN! PUT THAT DOWN!
WREN! PICK UP THOSE TOYS!
EAT YOUR SUPPER, WREN!
SHORT, CUTE AND WORKS WELL WITH A HOLLER, I'M SOLD.
♪ HELLO, WREN. ♪
KIRKMAN & SCOTT

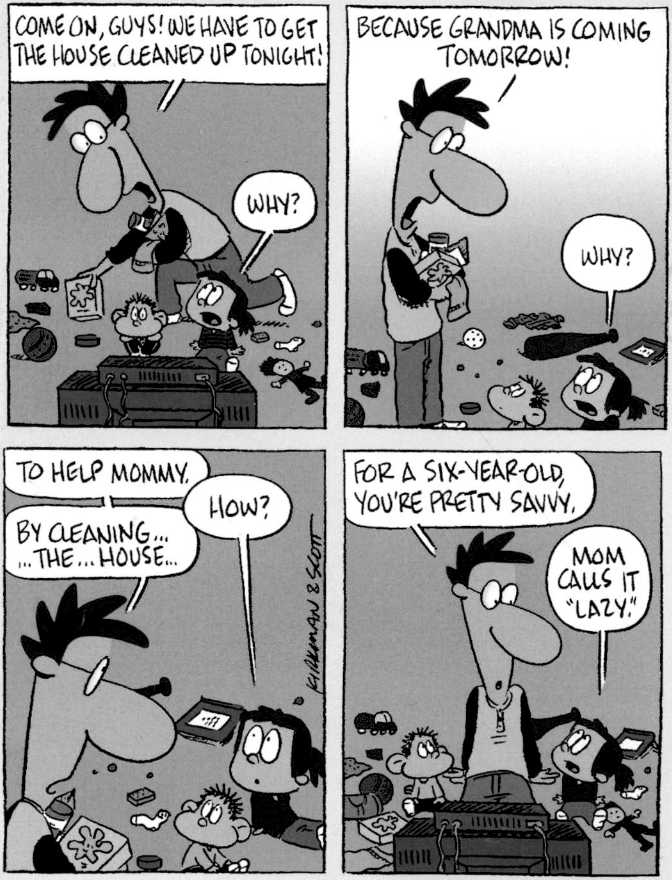
COME ON, GUYS! WE HAVE TO GET THE HOUSE CLEANED UP TONIGHT!
WHY?
BECAUSE GRANDMA IS COMING TOMORROW!
WHY?
TO HELP MOMMY.
HOW?
BY CLEANING... ...THE... HOUSE...
KIRKMAN & SCOTT
FOR A SIX-YEAR-OLD, YOU'RE PRETTY SAVVY.
MOM CALLS IT "LAZY."

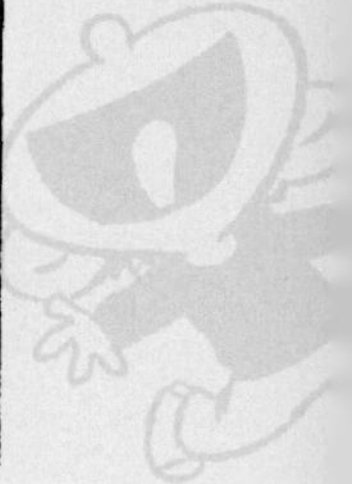

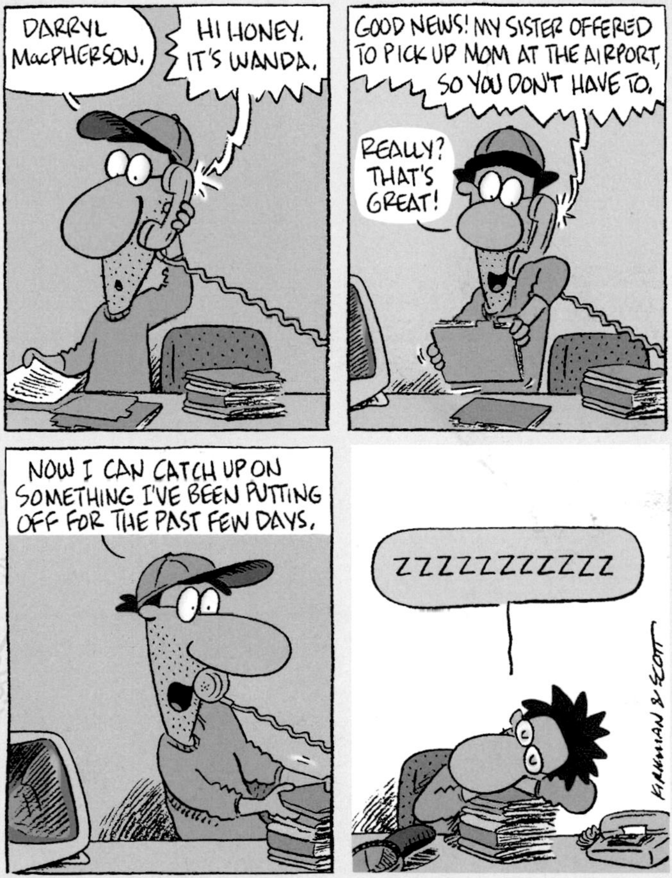
DARRYL MacPHERSON.
HI HONEY. IT'S WANDA.
GOOD NEWS! MY SISTER OFFERED TO PICK UP MOM AT THE AIRPORT, SO YOU DON'T HAVE TO.
REALLY? THAT'S GREAT!
NOW I CAN CATCH UP ON SOMETHING I'VE BEEN PUTTING OFF FOR THE PAST FEW DAYS.
ZZZZZZZZZZZZ
KIRKMAN & SCOTT

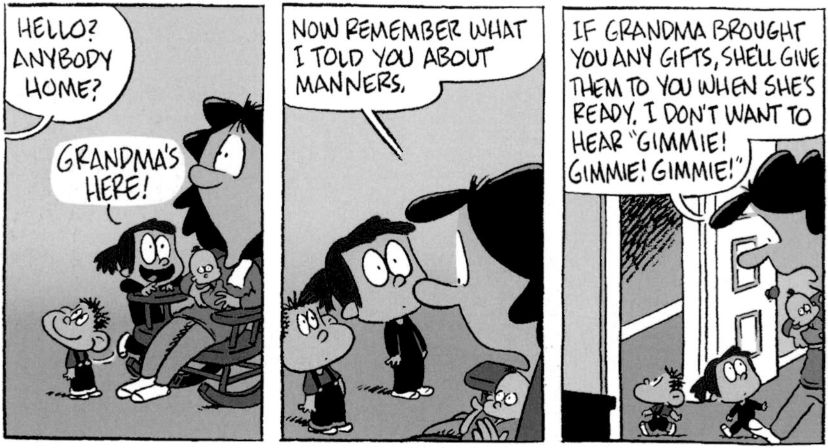
HELLO? ANYBODY HOME?
GRANDMA'S HERE!
NOW REMEMBER WHAT I TOLD YOU ABOUT MANNERS.
IF GRANDMA BROUGHT YOU ANY GIFTS, SHE'LL GIVE THEM TO YOU WHEN SHE'S READY. I DON'T WANT TO HEAR "GIMMIE! GIMMIE! GIMMIE!"

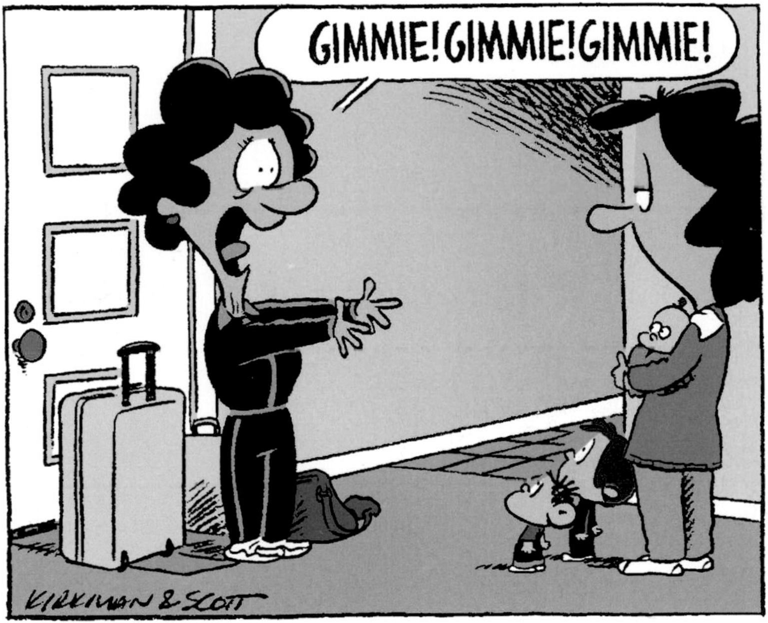
GIMMIE! GIMMIE! GIMMIE!
KIRKMAN & SCOTT

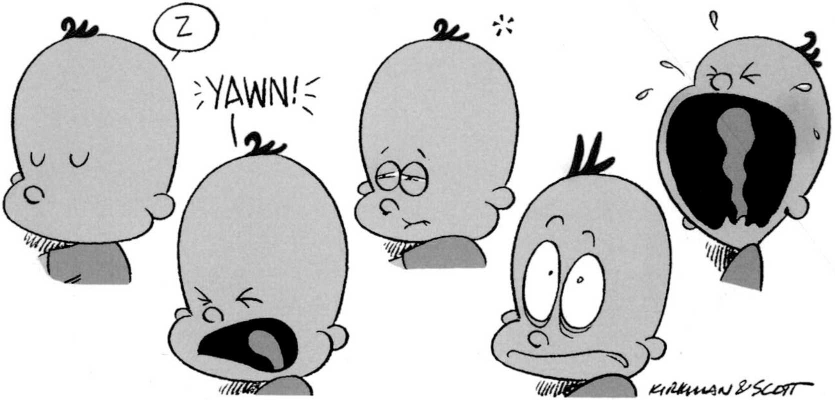
Z
YAWN!
KIRKMAN & SCOTT

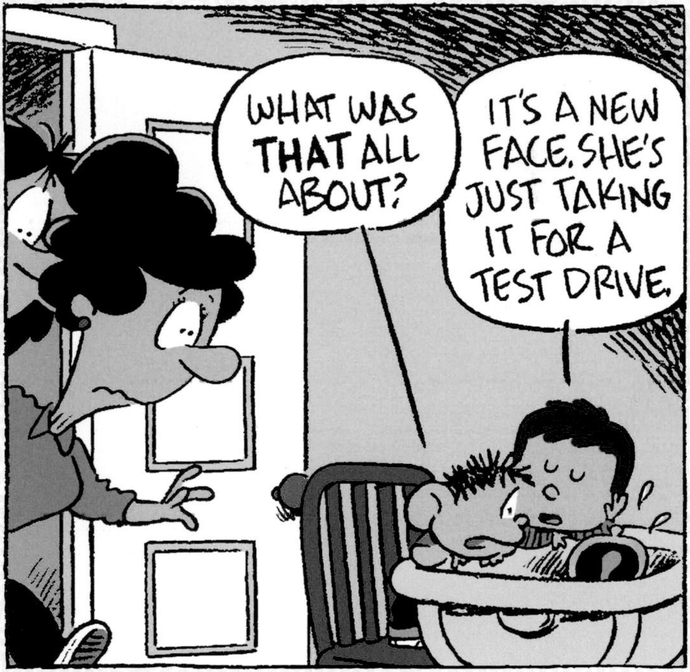
WHAT WAS **THAT** ALL ABOUT?
IT'S A NEW FACE. SHE'S JUST TAKING IT FOR A TEST DRIVE.

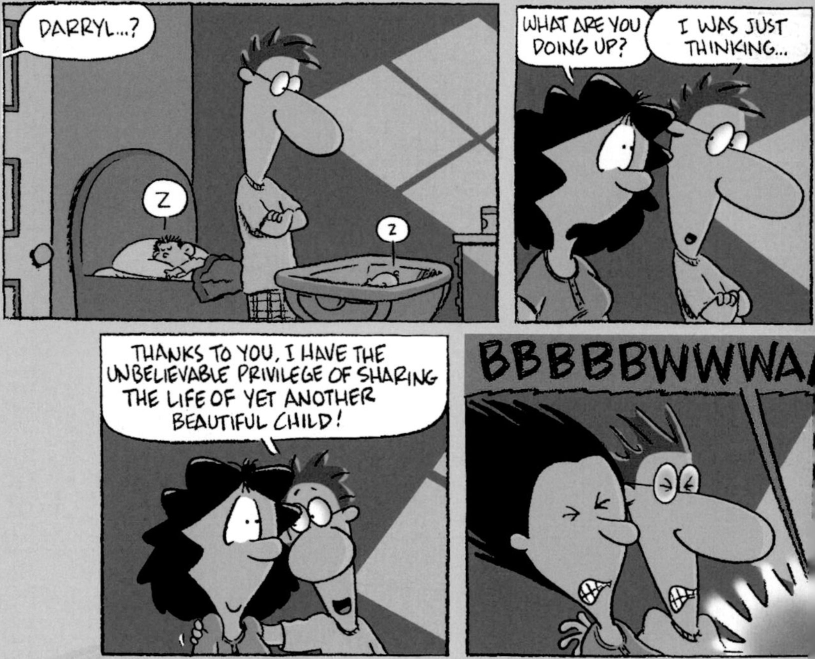
DARRYL...?
Z
Z
WHAT ARE YOU DOING UP?
I WAS JUST THINKING...
THANKS TO YOU, I HAVE THE UNBELIEVABLE PRIVILEGE OF SHARING THE LIFE OF YET ANOTHER BEAUTIFUL CHILD!
BBBBBWWWA

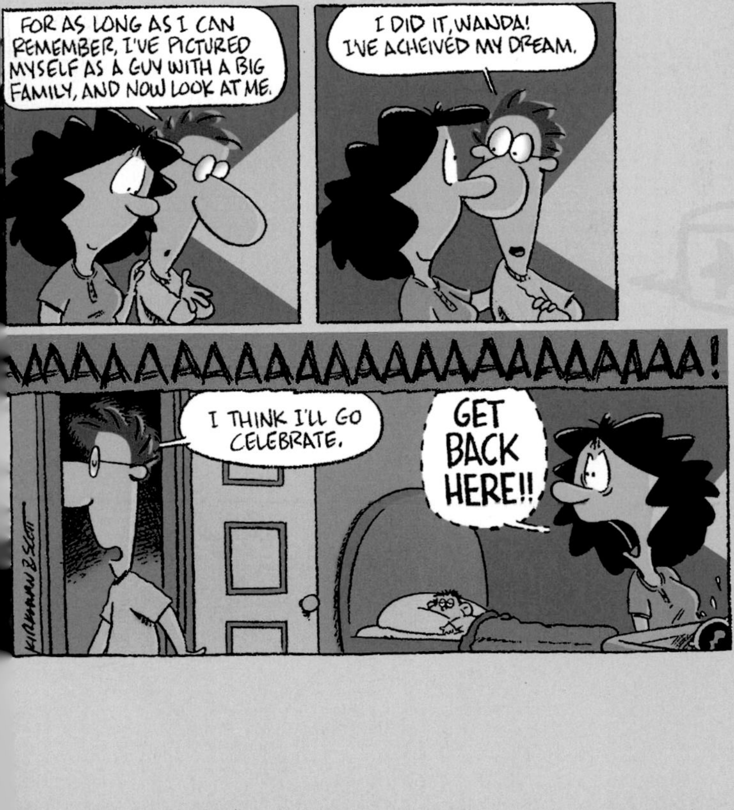
FOR AS LONG AS I CAN REMEMBER, I'VE PICTURED MYSELF AS A GUY WITH A BIG FAMILY, AND NOW LOOK AT ME.
I DID IT, WANDA! I'VE ACHEIVED MY DREAM.
WAAAAAAAAAAAAAAAAAAAAAA!
I THINK I'LL GO CELEBRATE.
GET BACK HERE!!
KIRKMAN & SCOTT

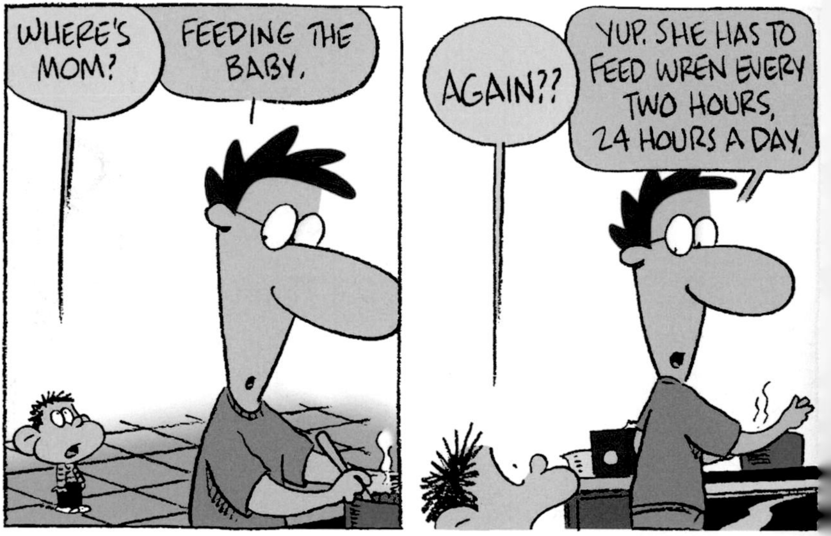
WHERE'S MOM?
FEEDING THE BABY.
AGAIN??
YUP. SHE HAS TO FEED WREN EVERY TWO HOURS, 24 HOURS A DAY.

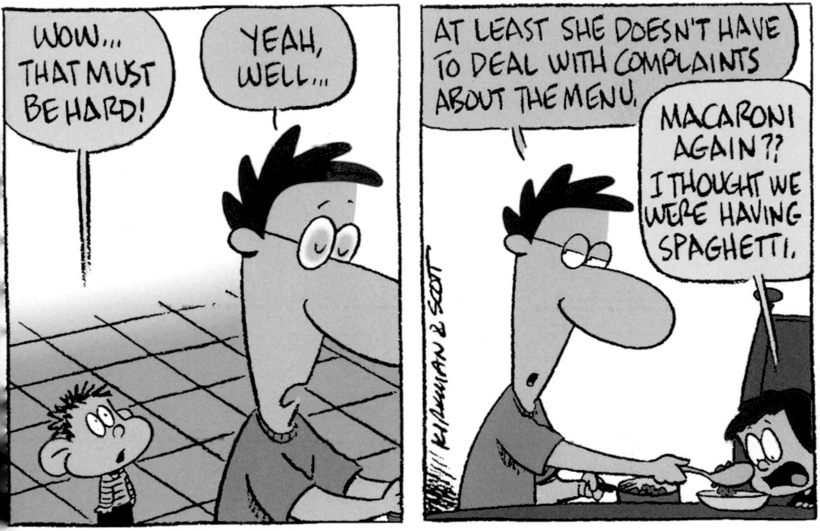
WOW... THAT MUST BE HARD!
YEAH, WELL...
AT LEAST SHE DOESN'T HAVE TO DEAL WITH COMPLAINTS ABOUT THE MENU.
MACARONI AGAIN?? I THOUGHT WE WERE HAVING SPAGHETTI.
KIRKMAN & SCOTT

CHAPTER 3

SIBLINGS

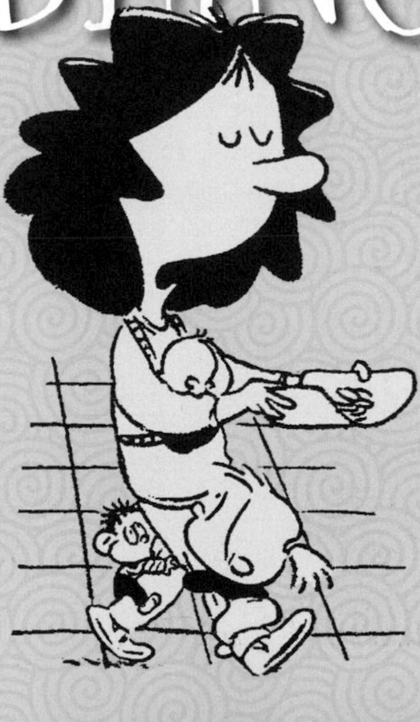

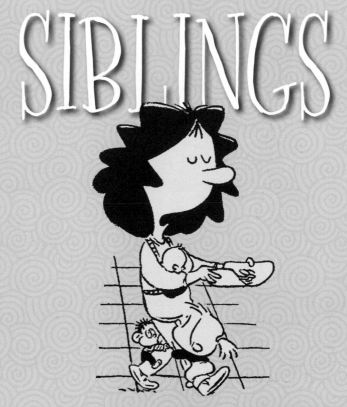

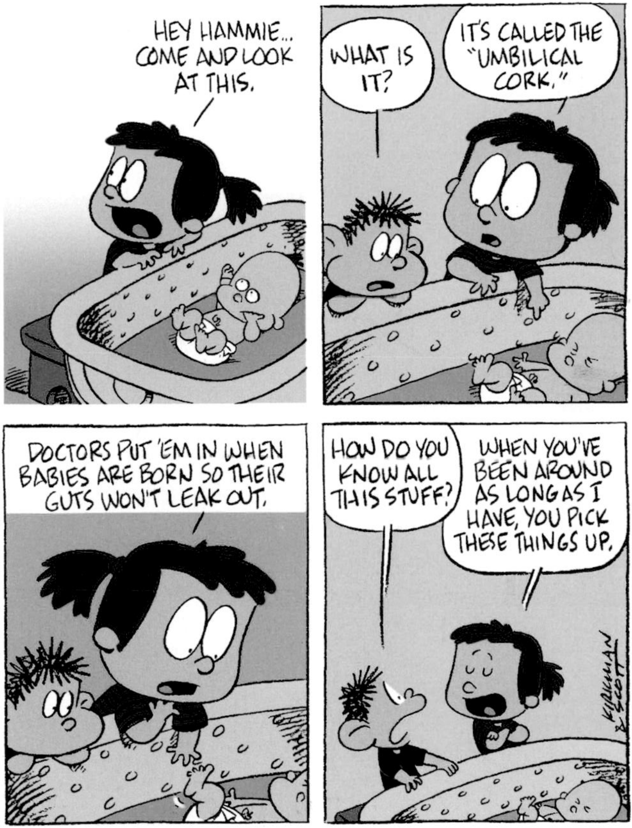
HEY HAMMIE... COME AND LOOK AT THIS.
WHAT IS IT?
IT'S CALLED THE "UMBILICAL CORK."
DOCTORS PUT 'EM IN WHEN BABIES ARE BORN SO THEIR GUTS WON'T LEAK OUT.
HOW DO YOU KNOW ALL THIS STUFF?
WHEN YOU'VE BEEN AROUND AS LONG AS I HAVE, YOU PICK THESE THINGS UP.
KIRKMAN & SCOTT

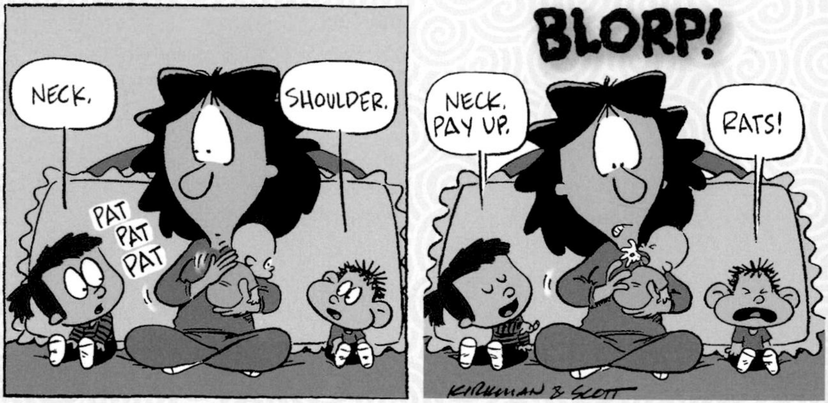
NECK.
SHOULDER.
PAT PAT PAT
BLORP!
NECK. PAY UP.
RATS!
KIRKMAN & SCOTT

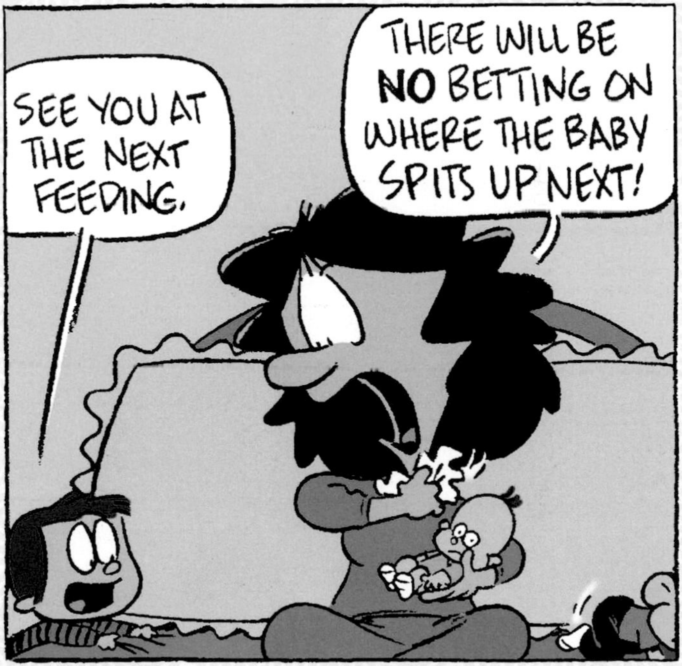
SEE YOU AT THE NEXT FEEDING.
THERE WILL BE **NO** BETTING ON WHERE THE BABY SPITS UP NEXT!

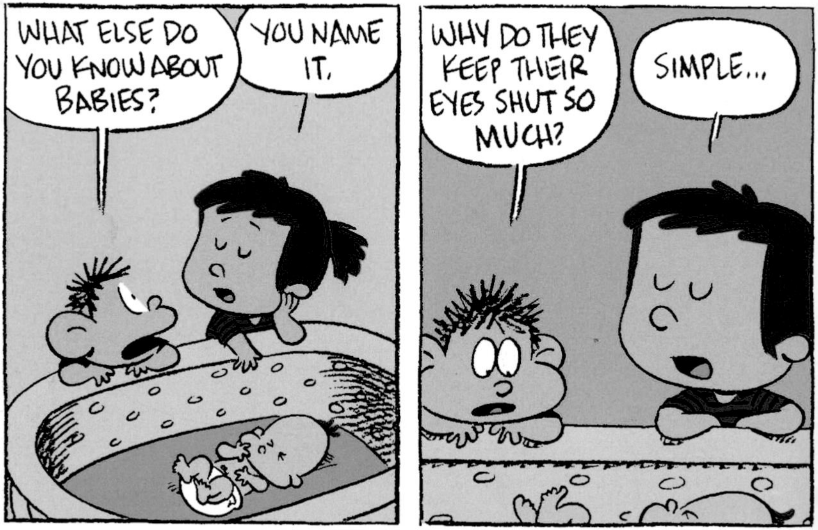
WHAT ELSE DO YOU KNOW ABOUT BABIES?
YOU NAME IT.
WHY DO THEY KEEP THEIR EYES SHUT SO MUCH?
SIMPLE...

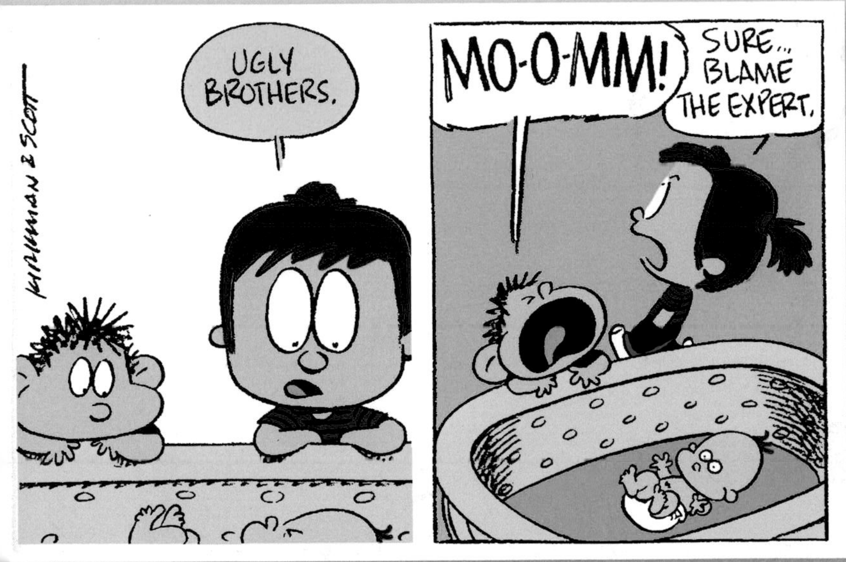
KIRKMAN & SCOTT
UGLY BROTHERS.
MO-O-MM!
SURE... BLAME THE EXPERT.

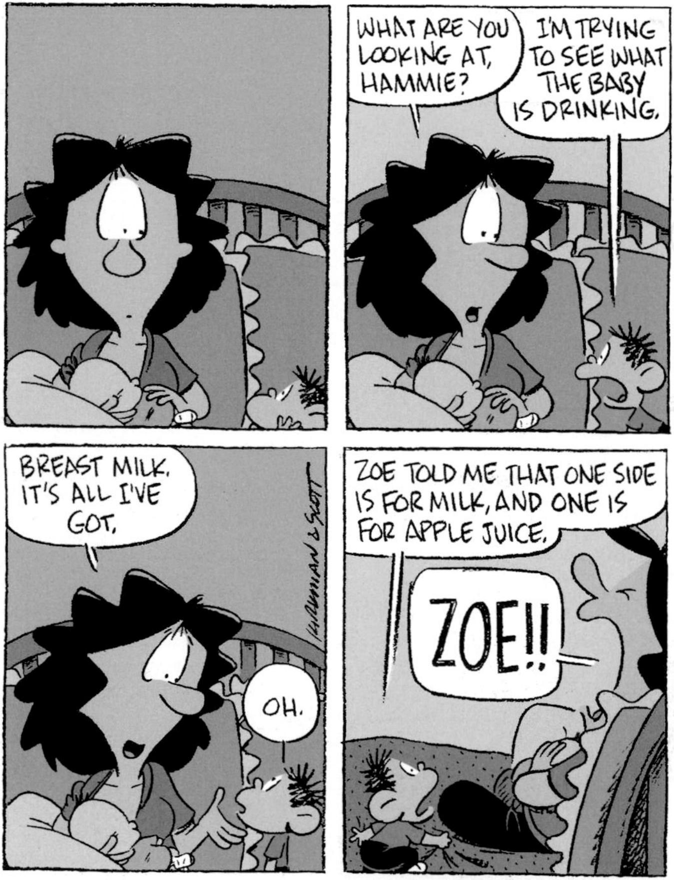
WHAT ARE YOU LOOKING AT, HAMMIE?
I'M TRYING TO SEE WHAT THE BABY IS DRINKING.
BREAST MILK. IT'S ALL I'VE GOT.
OH.
KIRKMAN & SCOTT
ZOE TOLD ME THAT ONE SIDE IS FOR MILK, AND ONE IS FOR APPLE JUICE.
ZOE!!

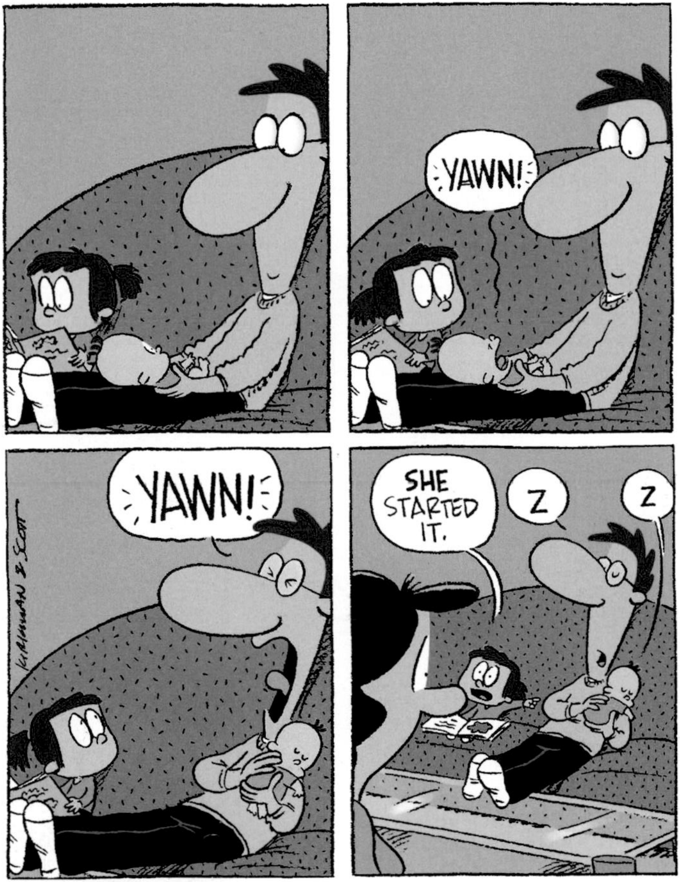
YAWN!
YAWN!
KIRKMAN & SCOTT
SHE STARTED IT.
Z
Z

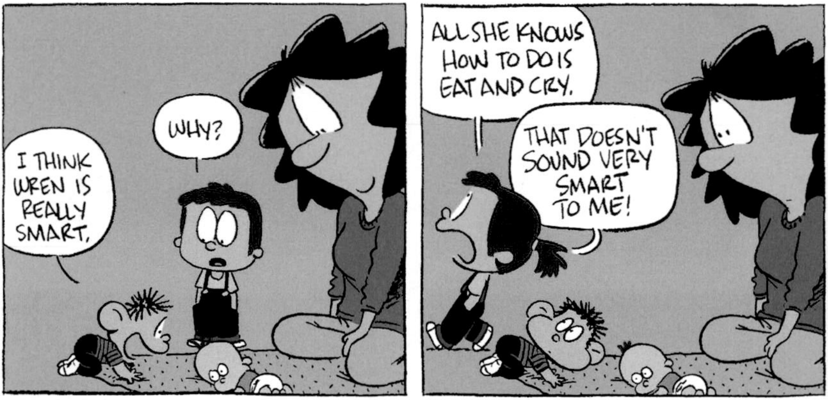
I THINK WREN IS REALLY SMART.
WHY?
ALL SHE KNOWS HOW TO DO IS EAT AND CRY.
THAT DOESN'T SOUND VERY SMART TO ME!

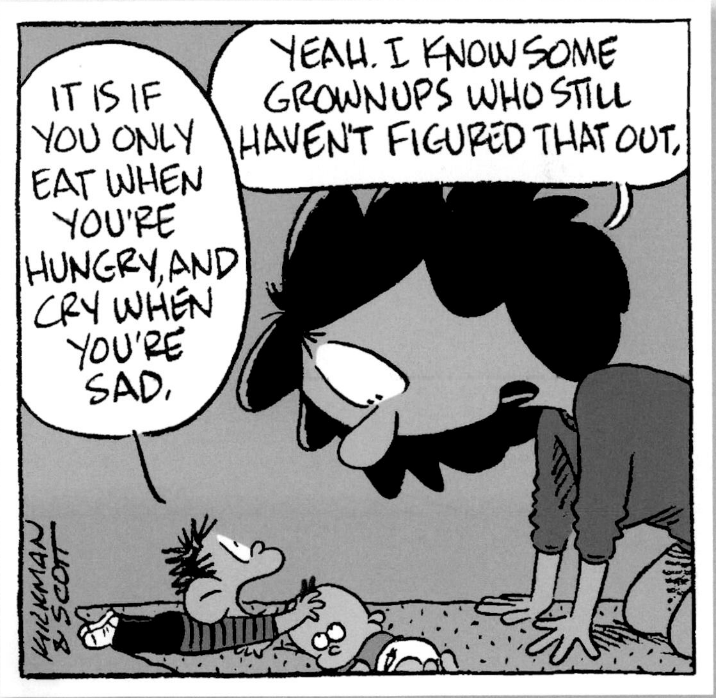
IT IS IF YOU ONLY EAT WHEN YOU'RE HUNGRY, AND CRY WHEN YOU'RE SAD.
YEAH. I KNOW SOME GROWNUPS WHO STILL HAVEN'T FIGURED THAT OUT.
KIRKMAN & SCOTT

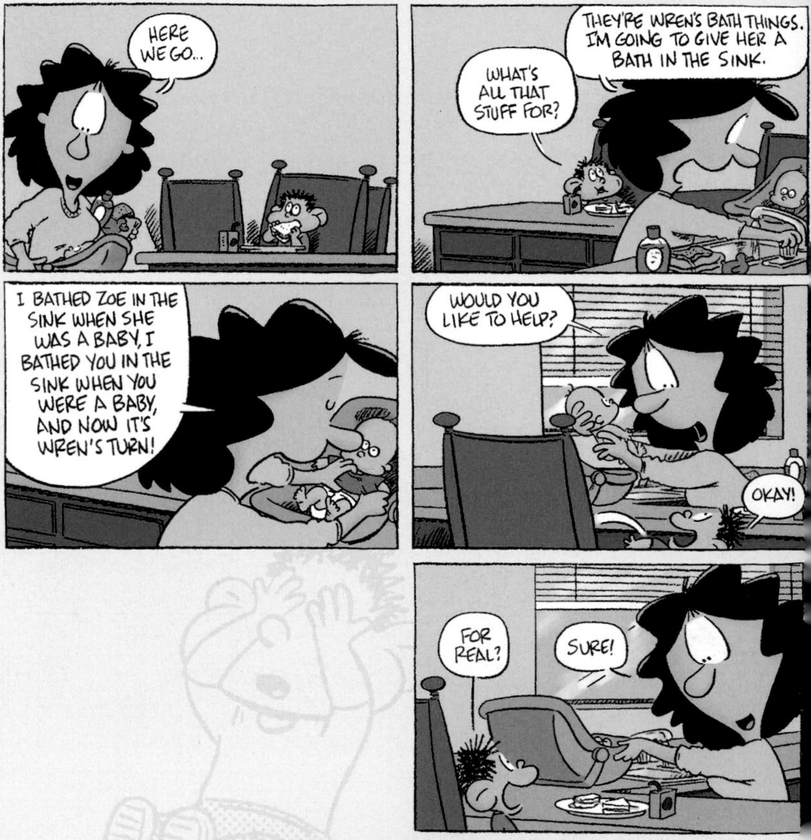
HERE WE GO...
WHAT'S ALL THAT STUFF FOR?
THEY'RE WREN'S BATH THINGS. I'M GOING TO GIVE HER A BATH IN THE SINK.
I BATHED ZOE IN THE SINK WHEN SHE WAS A BABY, I BATHED YOU IN THE SINK WHEN YOU WERE A BABY, AND NOW IT'S WREN'S TURN!
WOULD YOU LIKE TO HELP?
OKAY!
FOR REAL?
SURE!

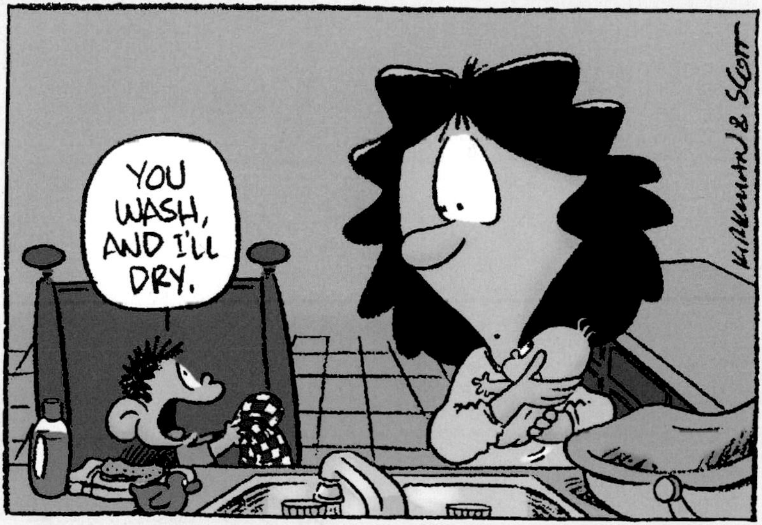
YOU WASH, AND I'LL DRY.
KIRKMAN & SCOTT

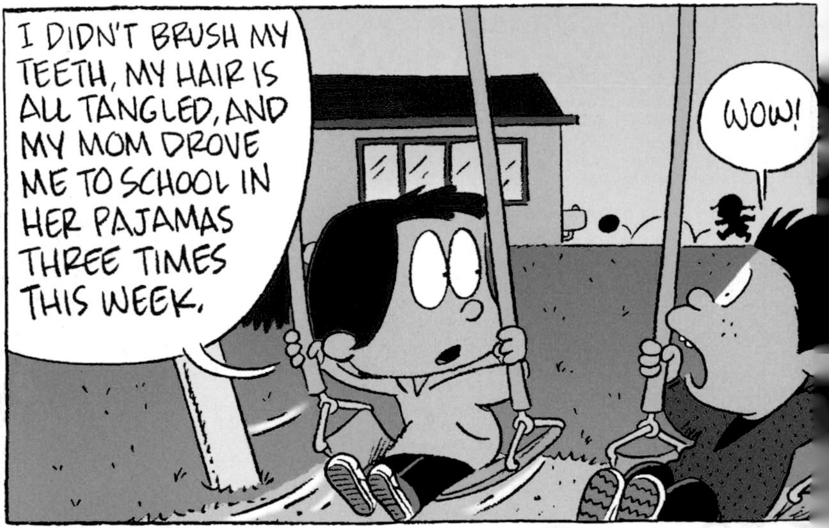
I DIDN'T BRUSH MY TEETH, MY HAIR IS ALL TANGLED, AND MY MOM DROVE ME TO SCHOOL IN HER PAJAMAS THREE TIMES THIS WEEK.
WOW!

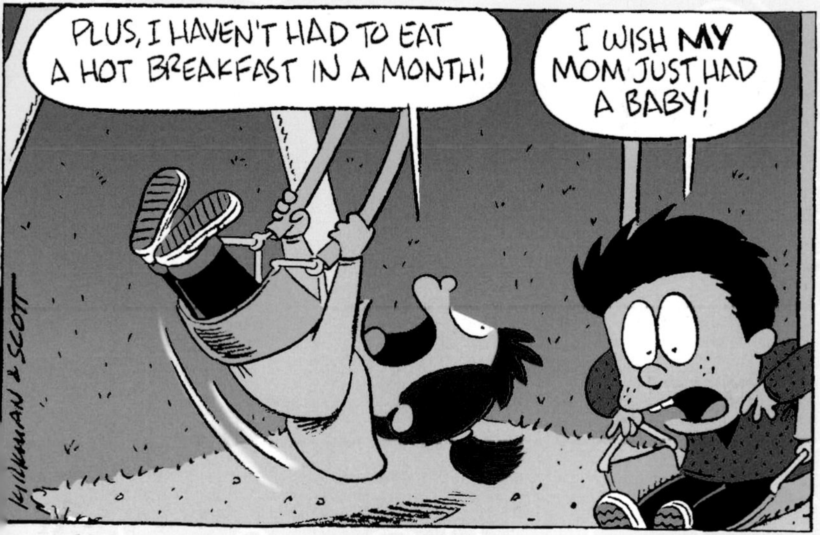
PLUS, I HAVEN'T HAD TO EAT A HOT BREAKFAST IN A MONTH!
I WISH MY MOM JUST HAD A BABY!
KIRKMAN & SCOTT

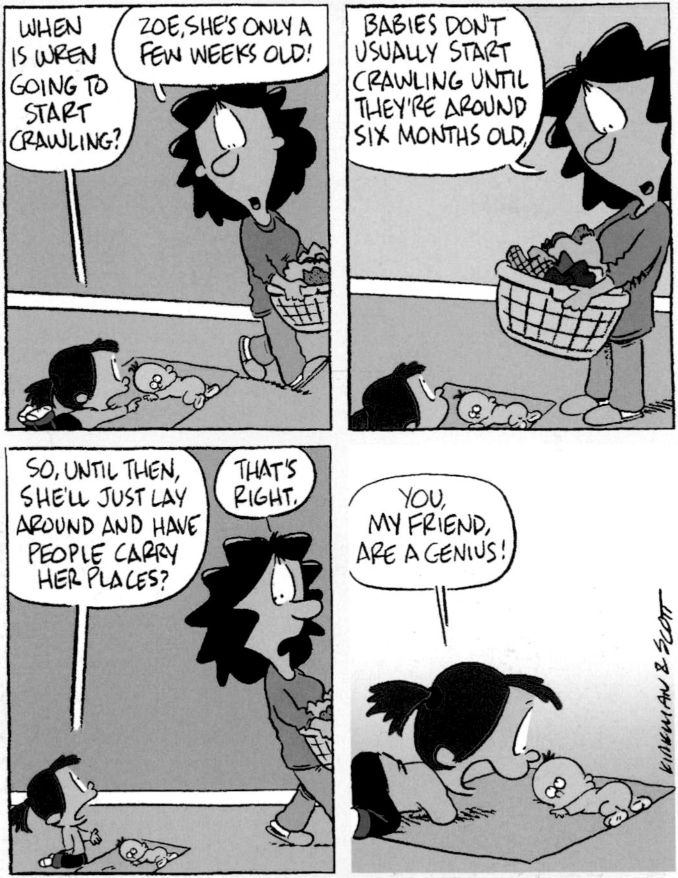
WHEN IS WREN GOING TO START CRAWLING?
ZOE, SHE'S ONLY A FEW WEEKS OLD!
BABIES DON'T USUALLY START CRAWLING UNTIL THEY'RE AROUND SIX MONTHS OLD.
SO, UNTIL THEN, SHE'LL JUST LAY AROUND AND HAVE PEOPLE CARRY HER PLACES?
THAT'S RIGHT.
YOU, MY FRIEND, ARE A GENIUS!
KIRKMAN & SCOTT

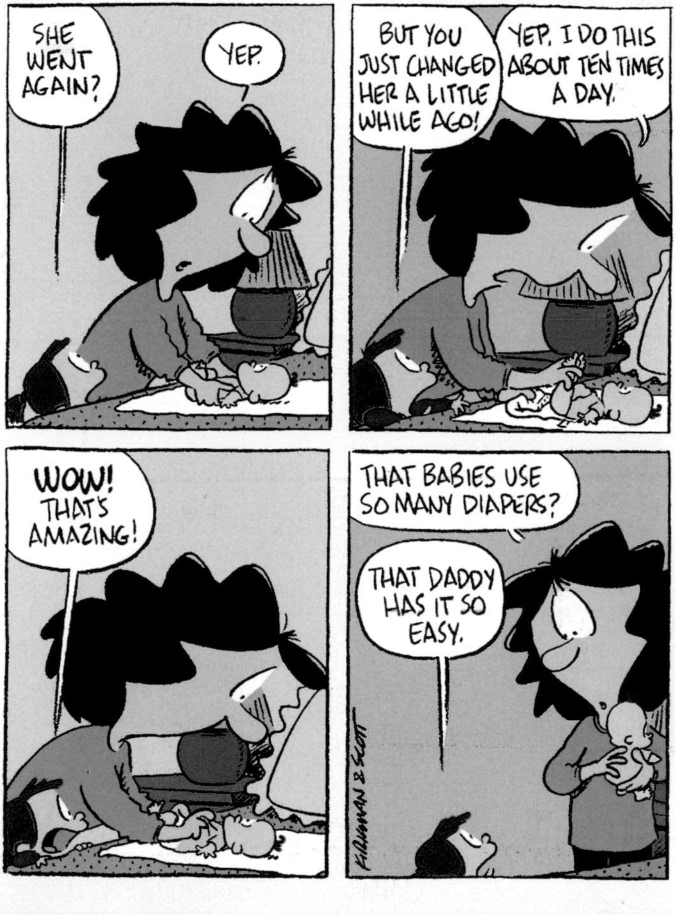
SHE WENT AGAIN?
YEP.
BUT YOU JUST CHANGED HER A LITTLE WHILE AGO!
YEP. I DO THIS ABOUT TEN TIMES A DAY.
WOW! THAT'S AMAZING!
THAT BABIES USE SO MANY DIAPERS?
THAT DADDY HAS IT SO EASY.
KIRKMAN & SCOTT

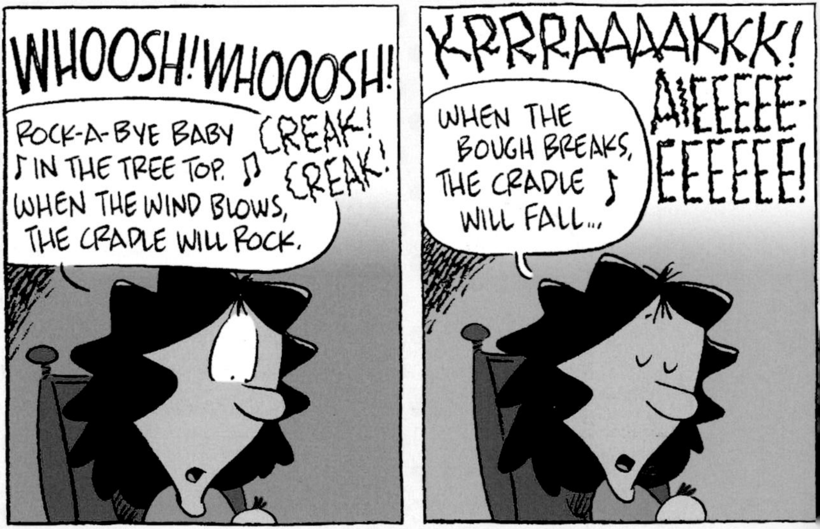
WHOOSH! WHOOOSH!
ROCK-A-BYE BABY ♪ IN THE TREE TOP. ♫ WHEN THE WIND BLOWS, THE CRADLE WILL ROCK.
CREAK! CREAK!
KRRRAAAAKKK!
WHEN THE BOUGH BREAKS, THE CRADLE ♪ WILL FALL...
AIEEEEE-EEEEEE!

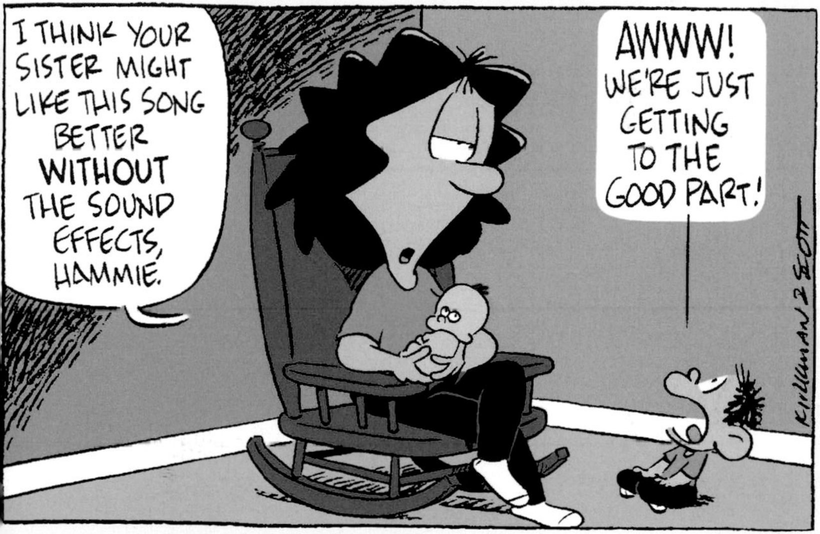
I THINK YOUR SISTER MIGHT LIKE THIS SONG BETTER WITHOUT THE SOUND EFFECTS, HAMMIE.
AWWW! WE'RE JUST GETTING TO THE GOOD PART!
KIRKMAN & SCOTT

CHAPTER 4

NEW ROUTINE

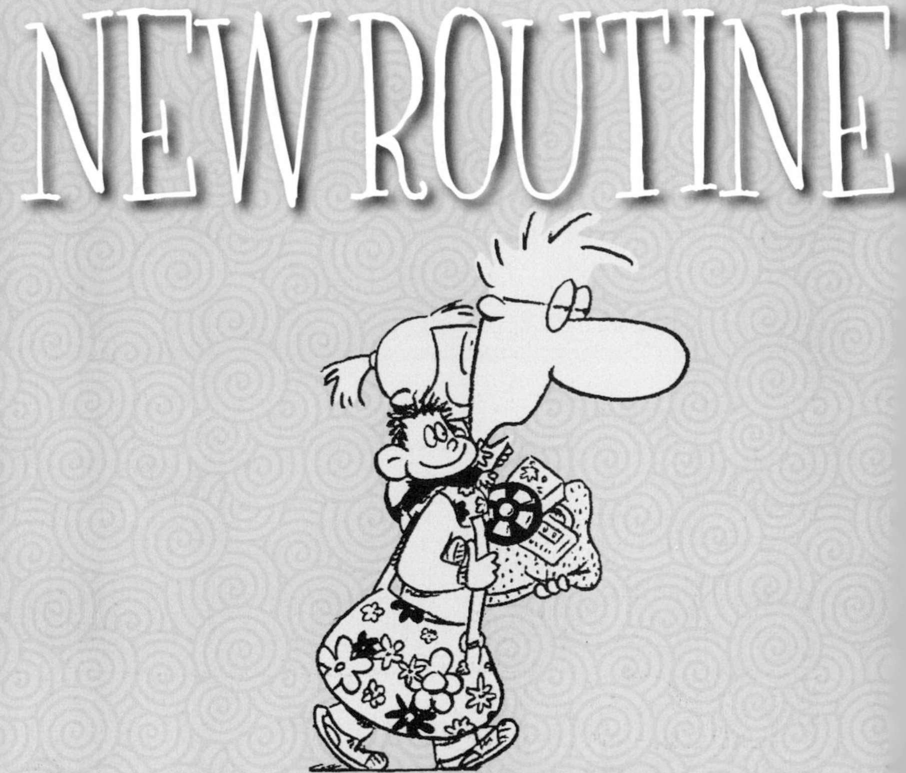

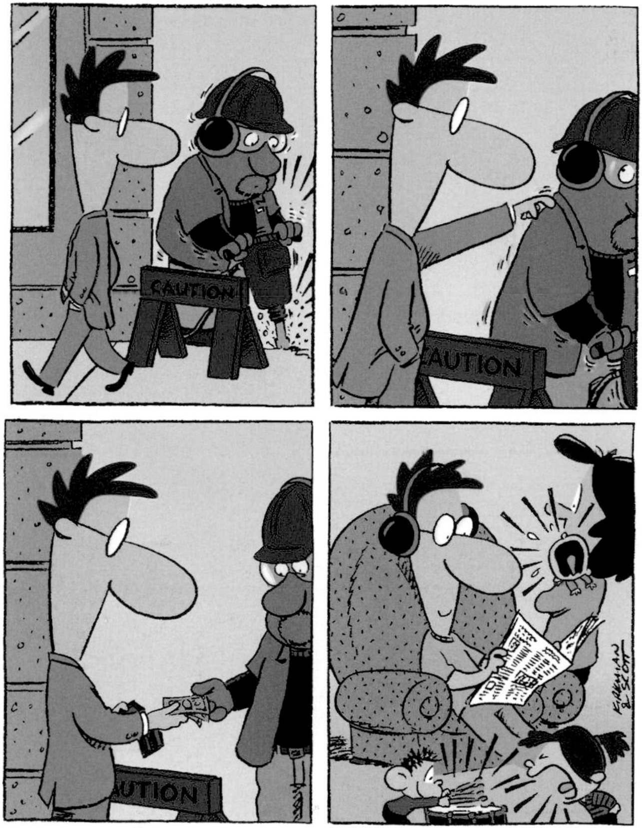
CAUTION
AUTION
AUTION
KIRKMAN & SCOTT

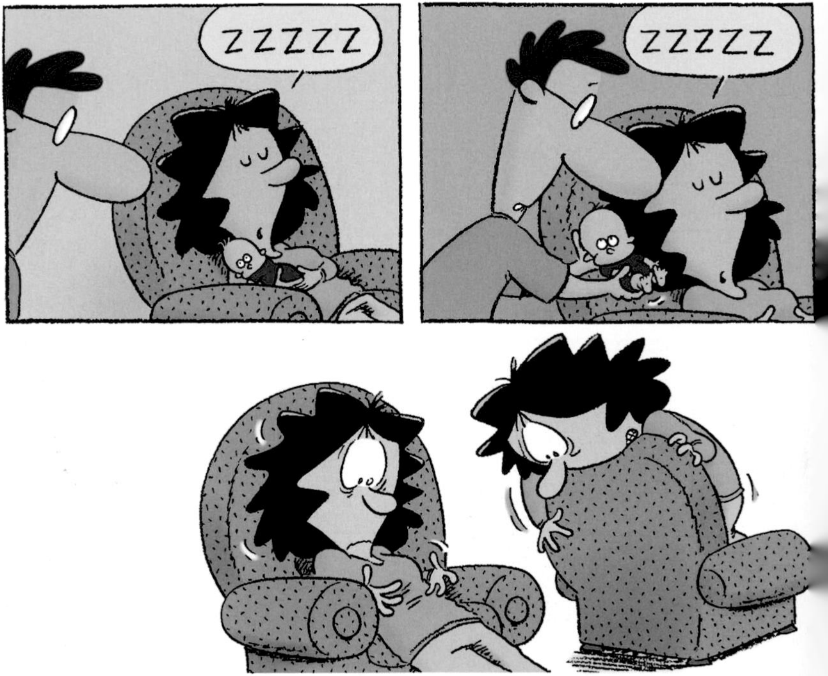
ZZZZZ
ZZZZZ

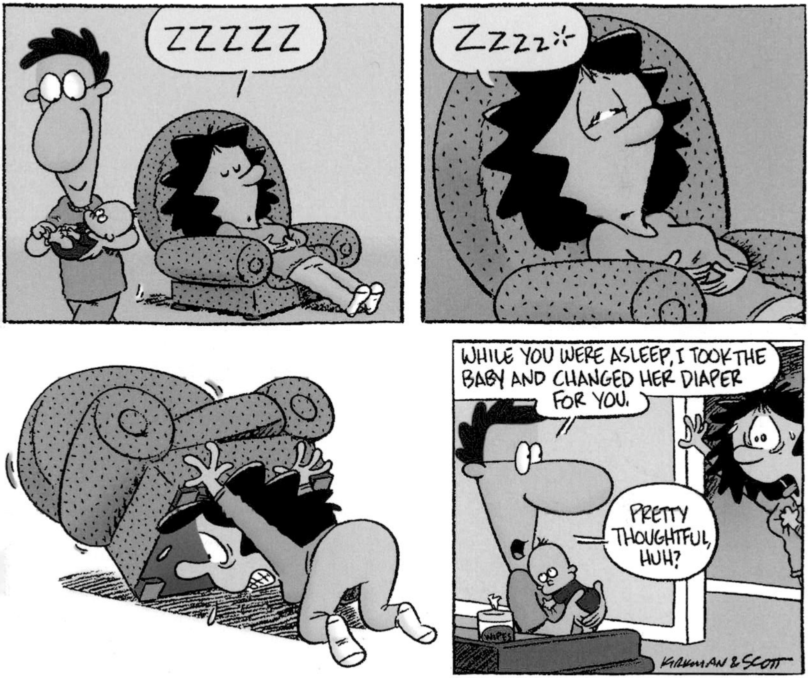
ZZZZZ
Zzzz
WHILE YOU WERE ASLEEP, I TOOK THE BABY AND CHANGED HER DIAPER FOR YOU.
PRETTY THOUGHTFUL, HUH?
WIPES
KIRKMAN & SCOTT

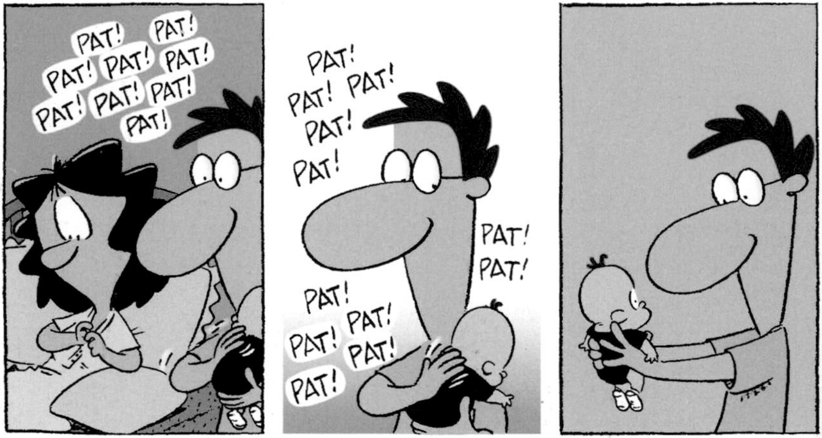
PAT! PAT!
PAT! PAT! PAT!
PAT! PAT! PAT!
PAT!
PAT!
PAT! PAT!
PAT!
PAT!
PAT!
PAT!
PAT!
PAT! PAT!
PAT! PAT!
PAT!

BLURP!

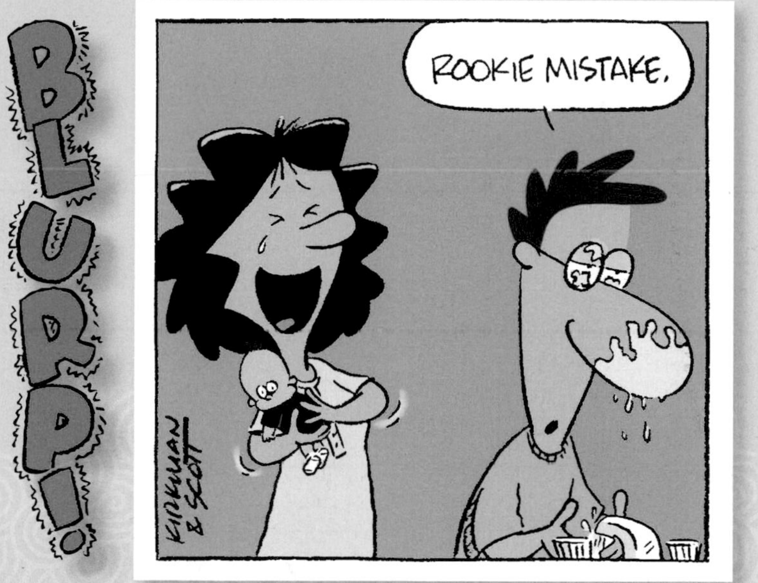
ROOKIE MISTAKE.
KIRKMAN & SCOTT

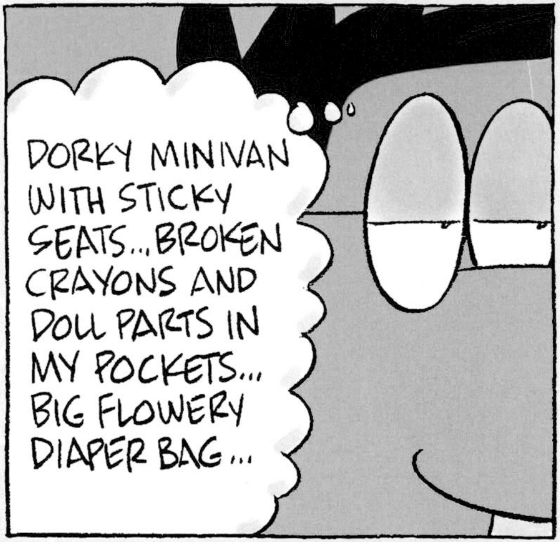
DORKY MINIVAN WITH STICKY SEATS...BROKEN CRAYONS AND DOLL PARTS IN MY POCKETS... BIG FLOWERY DIAPER BAG...

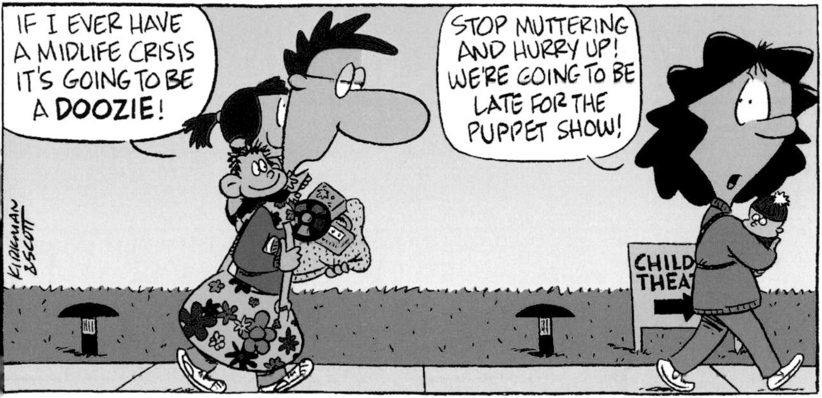
IF I EVER HAVE A MIDLIFE CRISIS IT'S GOING TO BE A **DOOZIE**!
STOP MUTTERING AND HURRY UP! WE'RE GOING TO BE LATE FOR THE PUPPET SHOW!
KIRKMAN & SCOTT
CHILD THEAT

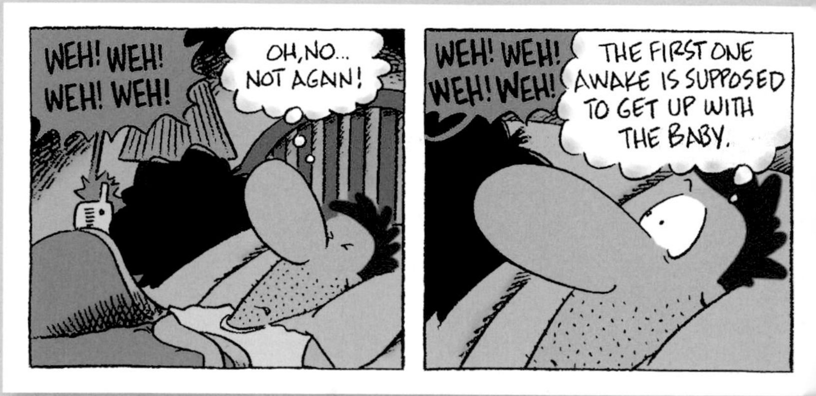
WEH! WEH! WEH! WEH!
OH, NO... NOT AGAIN!
WEH! WEH! WEH! WEH!
THE FIRST ONE AWAKE IS SUPPOSED TO GET UP WITH THE BABY.

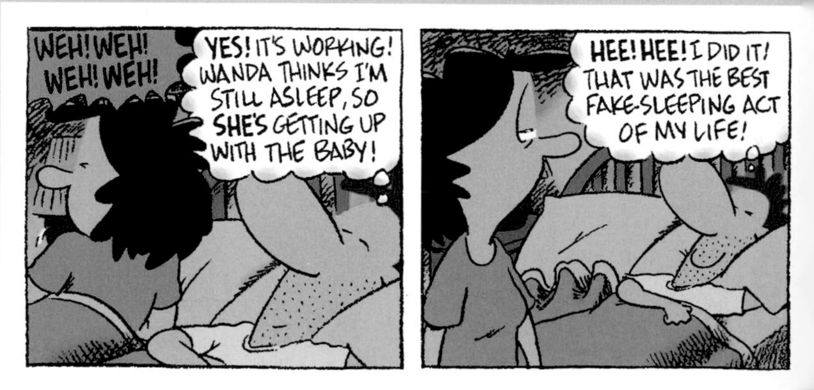
WEH! WEH! WEH! WEH!
YES! IT'S WORKING! WANDA THINKS I'M STILL ASLEEP, SO SHE'S GETTING UP WITH THE BABY!
HEE! HEE! I DID IT! THAT WAS THE BEST FAKE-SLEEPING ACT OF MY LIFE!

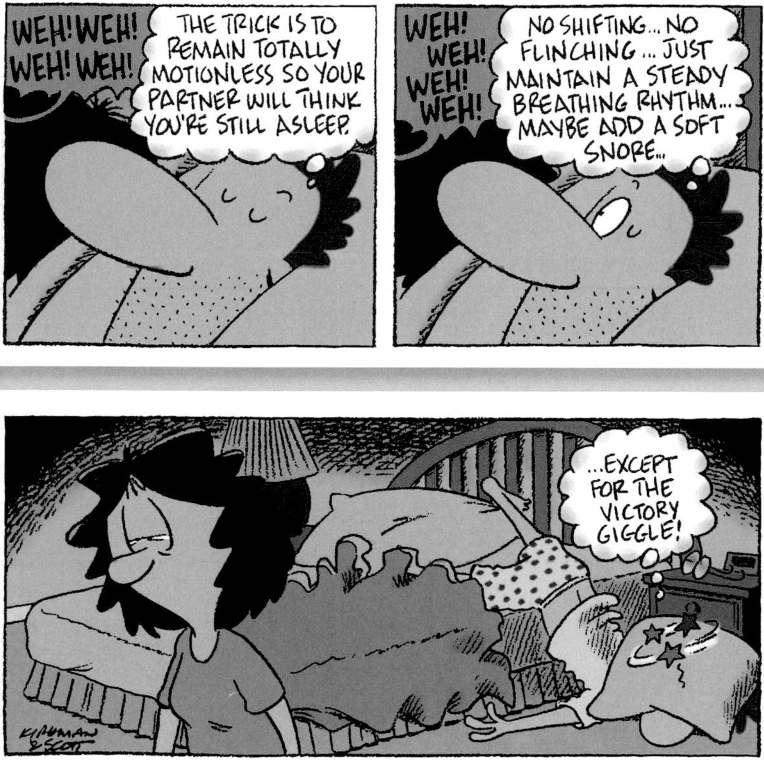
WEH! WEH! WEH! WEH!
THE TRICK IS TO REMAIN TOTALLY MOTIONLESS SO YOUR PARTNER WILL THINK YOU'RE STILL ASLEEP.
WEH! WEH! WEH! WEH!
NO SHIFTING... NO FLINCHING... JUST MAINTAIN A STEADY BREATHING RHYTHM... MAYBE ADD A SOFT SNORE...
...EXCEPT FOR THE VICTORY GIGGLE!
KIRKMAN & SCOTT

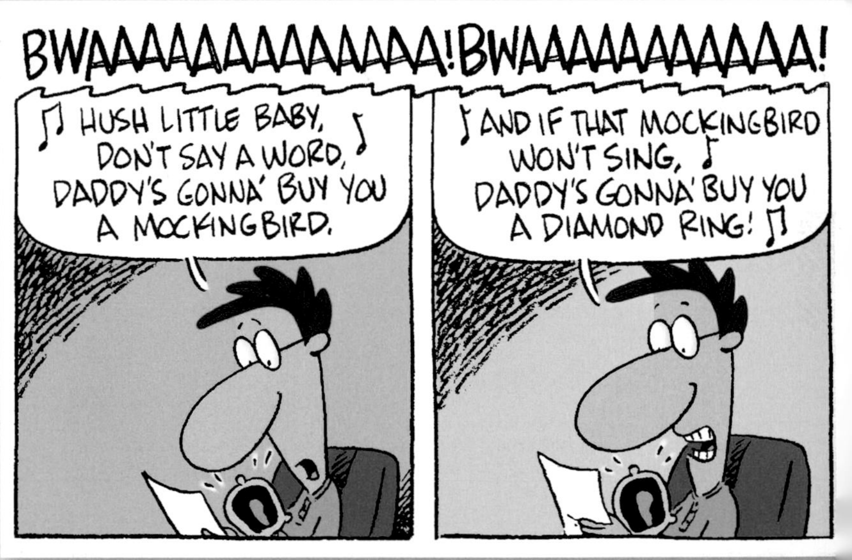
BWAAAAAAAAAAAAAA! BWAAAAAAAAAAAAA!
HUSH LITTLE BABY, DON'T SAY A WORD, DADDY'S GONNA' BUY YOU A MOCKINGBIRD.
AND IF THAT MOCKINGBIRD WON'T SING, DADDY'S GONNA' BUY YOU A DIAMOND RING!

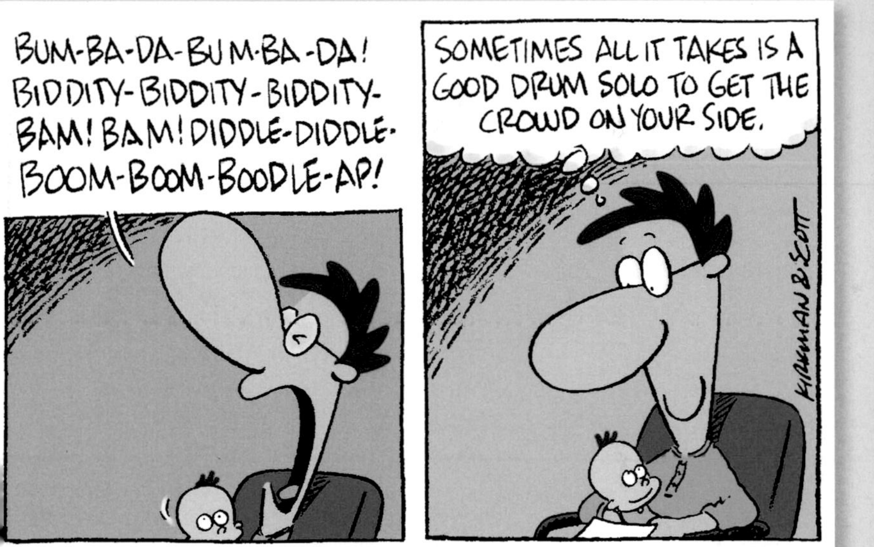

BUM-BA-DA-BUM-BA-DA! BIDDITY-BIDDITY-BIDDITY-BAM! BAM! DIDDLE-DIDDLE-BOOM-BOOM-BOODLE-AP!
SOMETIMES ALL IT TAKES IS A GOOD DRUM SOLO TO GET THE CROWD ON YOUR SIDE.
KIRKMAN & SCOTT

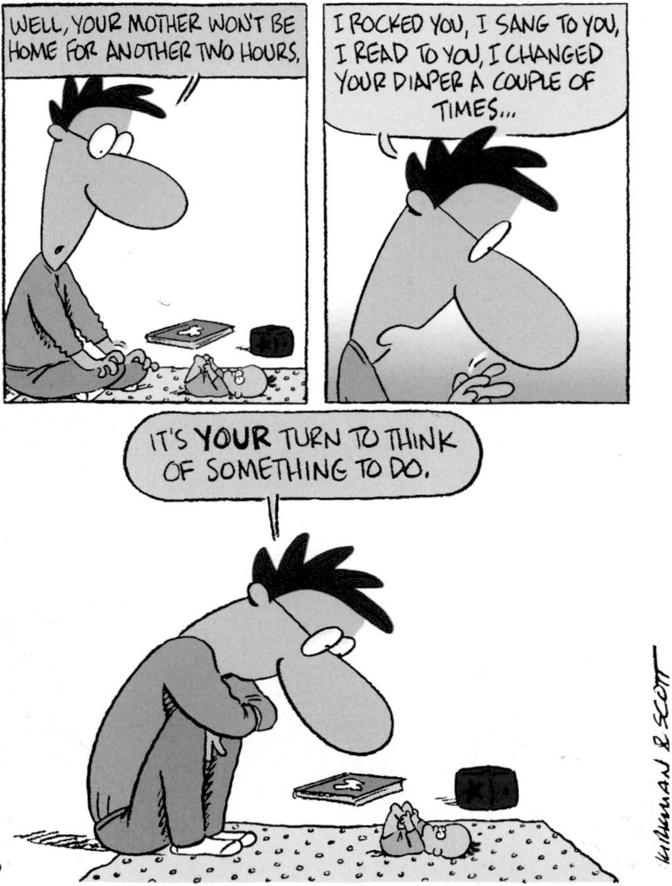
WELL, YOUR MOTHER WON'T BE HOME FOR ANOTHER TWO HOURS.
I ROCKED YOU, I SANG TO YOU, I READ TO YOU, I CHANGED YOUR DIAPER A COUPLE OF TIMES...
IT'S **YOUR** TURN TO THINK OF SOMETHING TO DO.
KIRKMAN & SCOTT

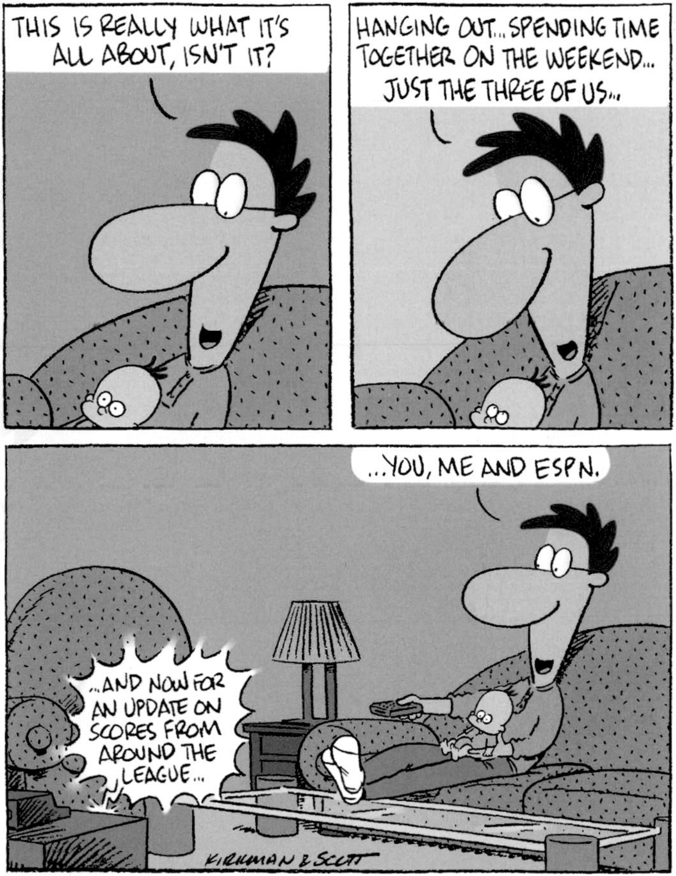
THIS IS REALLY WHAT IT'S ALL ABOUT, ISN'T IT?
HANGING OUT...SPENDING TIME TOGETHER ON THE WEEKEND... JUST THE THREE OF US...
...YOU, ME AND ESPN.
...AND NOW FOR AN UPDATE ON SCORES FROM AROUND THE LEAGUE...
KIRKMAN & SCOTT

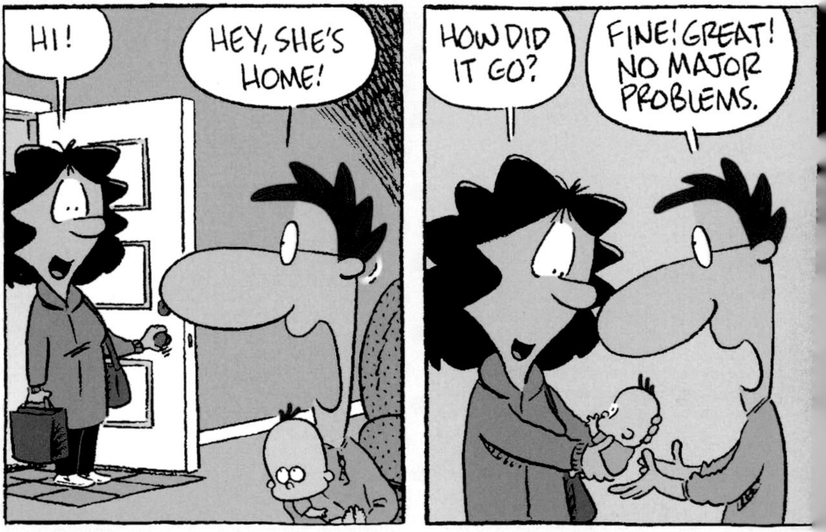
HI!
HEY, SHE'S HOME!
HOW DID IT GO?
FINE! GREAT! NO MAJOR PROBLEMS.

KISS! CHALK UP ANOTHER ROUND OF EXCELLENT PARENTING FOR DARRYL MacPHERSON!
KIRKMAN & SCOTT
HOW COME WHEN **YOU** STAY HOME WITH THE KIDS IT'S CALLED "**PARENTING**," AND WHEN **I** STAY HOME WITH THE KIDS IT'S CALLED "**NOT WORKING**"??

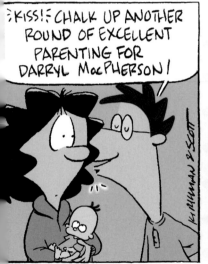

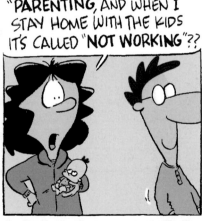